WHERE I LIVE

By TENNESSEE WILLIAMS

PLAYS

Baby Doll (a screenplay)
Camino Real
Cat on a Hot Tin Roof
Dragon Country
The Glass Menagerie
Out Cry
Period of Adjustment
Small Craft Warnings
A Streetcar Named Desire
Sweet Bird of Youth

THE THEATRE OF TENNESSEE WILLIAMS, VOLUME I
   Battle of Angels
   A Streetcar Named Desire
   The Glass Menagerie

THE THEATRE OF TENNESSEE WILLIAMS, VOLUME II
   The Eccentricities of a Nightingale
   Summer and Smoke
   The Rose Tattoo
   Camino Real

THE THEATRE OF TENNESSEE WILLIAMS, VOLUME III
   Cat on a Hot Tin Roof
   Orpheus Descending
   Suddenly Last Summer

THE THEATRE OF TENNESSEE WILLIAMS, VOLUME IV
   Sweet Bird of Youth
   Period of Adjustment
   The Night of the Iguana

THE THEATRE OF TENNESSEE WILLIAMS, VOLUME V
   The Milk Train Doesn't Stop Here Anymore
   Kingdom of Earth
     (The Seven Descents of Myrtle)
   Small Craft Warnings
   The Two-Character Play
27 Wagons Full of Cotton and Other Plays

POETRY

Androgyne, Mon Amour
In the Winter of Cities

PROSE

Eight Mortal Ladies Possessed
Hard Candy and Other Stories
The Knightly Quest and Other Stories
One Arm and Other Stories
The Roman Spring of Mrs. Stone
Where I Live: Selected Essays

Where I Live

SELECTED ESSAYS

by Tennessee Williams

Edited by Christine R. Day and Bob Woods

With an Introduction by Christine R. Day

A NEW DIRECTIONS BOOK

Grateful acknowledgment is given to the editors and publishers of the following, in which some of the essays in this volume first appeared: Caedmon Records, *Five Young American Poets*, *Harper's Bazaar*, *Life*, *The London Observer*, *The New York Herald Tribune*, *The New York Star*, *The New York Times*, *Playbill*, *The Saturday Review of Literature*, and *Vogue*.

Manufactured in the United States of America
First published clothbound and as New Directions Paperbook 468 in 1978
Published simultaneously in Canada by McClelland & Stewart, Ltd.

Library of Congress Cataloging in Publication Data
Williams, Tennessee, 1911–
   Where I live.
   (A New Directions Book)
   I. Day, Christine R. II. Woods, Bob. III. Title.
PS3545.I5365W5   814'.5'4   78–19046
ISBN 0–8112–0705–6
ISBN 0–8112–0706–4 pbk.

New Directions Books are published for James Laughlin
by New Directions Publishing Corporation,
333 Sixth Avenue, New York 10014

Contents

Introduction:
Personal Lyricism

THIS SELECTION of essays chronicles the development, both personally and artistically, of a talented, perceptive and influential American playwright, Tennessee Williams. Born in his grandfather's Episcopal rectory in Columbus, Mississippi, Thomas Lanier Williams came, on his father's side, from pioneer Tennessee stock and, on his mother's paternal side, from Quakers who were Tories and fled to Canada during the American Revolution. Williams writes that "roughly there was a combination of Puritan and Cavalier strains in my blood which may be accountable for the conflicting impulses I often represent in the people I write about."

His first literary efforts were rewarded by applause and small prizes from literary and women's clubs. He tells us that most of this was "lyric poetry which was a bad imitation of Edna Millay." Later, feeling that these early attempts had compromised his name, he changed it to "Tennessee" Williams with "the justification being mainly that the Williamses had fought the Indians for Tennessee" and that he "had already discovered that the life of a young writer was going to be something similar to the defense of a stockade against a band of savages."

Although his talent as a playwright received what seemed to be overnight recognition with the New York production of *The Glass Menagerie* in 1945, Williams had been developing his theatrical skills for most of his life. During the Thirties and early Forties, academic pursuits alternated with a series of odd jobs in odd places. The University of Missouri gave way to Washington University in St. Louis and finally to the University of Iowa, from which he received a B.A. degree in 1938. Before, after, and in between, Williams worked as an elevator operator, a waiter at a small restaurant in New Orleans, a teletype operator in Florida, an usher at the Strand Theater on Broadway, and a squab picker on a pigeon ranch in California. And, like Tom in *The Glass Menagerie,* he wrote during the hours he was paid to devote to the International Shoe Company in St. Louis (which employed his father as sales manager at a different branch).

During this period, Williams wrote in every spare moment, but he also served his theatrical apprenticeship with several university, community, and small professional theater groups, including The Mummers of St. Louis which he describes in "Something Wild. . . ." Finally, in 1939, a collection of one-act plays, *American Blues,* won a special $100 prize from the Group Theatre, and, not long after, Williams received a $1,000 Rockefeller grant. With the Theatre Guild production of *Battle of Angels* in 1940, Williams became a "professional," even though the play closed after its Boston tryout. Later, in Hollywood, he earned the then fabulous salary of $250 per week writing scripts and dialogue for M-G-M, and the money he was able to save from that job sustained him while he wrote *The Glass Menagerie*.

With the production of *The Glass Menagerie*, Tennessee Williams became a major figure in the American theater. The story of a fading Southern belle, her shy daughter and restless son, this play transcended regionalism and brought to national attention Williams's rich understanding of the human psyche, his astute observation of character and behavior, and his unique sense of the theater and of storytelling.

As described in "On a Streetcar Named Success" and "If the Writing Is Honest," Williams reacted to his sudden fame with shock. Even during the Chicago tryout of *Menagerie*, he had retreated to his parents' home in St. Louis for temporary seclusion. In New York, after becoming more acclimated to the prosperity the play brought him, he moved to a first-class hotel. Again finding himself an easy target for opportunists, Williams isolated himself by going into the hospital; often plagued by serious bouts of ill health, he underwent cataract surgery at this time. His recovery from the operation paralleled a similar recovery in his faith in friends. From the hospital, Williams went to Mexico to recuperate and began work on a play originally called *The Poker Night,* known today as *A Streetcar Named Desire,* winner of a New York Drama Critics' Circle Award and a Pulitzer Prize.

This success was followed by a long series of plays, many prize-winning, which have uniformly become staples of the American dramatic repertoire: *Summer and Smoke, The Rose Tattoo, Camino Real, Cat on a Hot Tin Roof, Orpheus De-*

scending, *Suddenly Last Summer, Sweet Bird of Youth, Period of Adjustment, Night of the Iguana,* and more recently *Eccentricities of a Nightingale, Small Craft Warnings,* and *The Two-Character Play. Vieux Carré* and *Crêve Coeur* are the latest additions to this impressive list.

But Tennessee Williams has also exhibited his talent in other genres. His short stories, which have provided seeds for some of his major plays, are available in several collections: *One Arm and Other Stories; Hard Candy: A Book of Stories; The Knightly Quest: A Novella and Four Short Stories;* and *Eight Mortal Ladies Possessed: A Book of Stories.* He has also published two novels: *The Roman Spring of Mrs. Stone* and *Moise and the World of Reason;* film scripts for *Baby Doll* and "Stop Rocking," as well as a film or television adaptation of his classic short story, "One Arm"; and the autobiographical *Memoirs.* His verse includes an early contribution to the New Directions series, *Five Young American Poets,* 1944 (whose introduction "Preface to My Poems" appears in this volume) and two collections, *In the Winter of Cities* and *Androgyne, Mon Amour.*

In each form of his artistry, Williams exhibits a simultaneous exuberance and intensity. This natural lyricism saw him through even in those difficult times in his early career when he was often on the verge of starvation; Williams reports that he kept on writing "not with any hope of making a living at it, but because I found no other means of expressing things that seemed to demand expression. There was never a moment when I did not find life to be immeasurably exciting to experience and to witness, however difficult it was to sustain."

Williams found that the pains and pleasures of humanity create a tension which must be housed in the body and the mind. To him, a person seems to ache continually with the exercise of existence, the effort of trying to resolve this tension. The difficulty of this resolution creates a violent energy of its own, which is channeled in as many ways as there are people. Tennessee Williams channels his energy into a lyricism evident in his work.

The essays included in this volume exhibit an extension of his artistic lyricism, a lyricism with a more personal emphasis. The form of an essay, necessarily, involves different artistic restraints than that of a play. In the theater, the members of the audience eavesdrop on Williams's plays as they sit safely "in a comforting dusk to watch a world which is flooded with light"; in these essays, the reader is addressed directly. Mr. Williams confides: "I want to go on talking to you as freely and intimately about what we live and die for as if I knew you better than anyone else whom you know." And he does just that. He writes to his reader—there is no pretentious exercise in ambiguity nor is there a struggle to see through a pair of one-way mirror sunglasses.

In these essays, in fluid language and on an intimately personal level, Tennessee Williams talks directly to his readers about love, rejection, death, friendship, hate, art, social pretensions, the isolation of the individual, the transience of our world, the conditional—and sometimes contradictory—nature of truth, childhood recollections, and the numerous other feelings and concepts with which we all must deal in our lives on whatever level we can. This directness thrusts the reader into the middle of a Van Gogh picture of Williams's life: you are there when he depicts the "ugly rows of apartment buildings the color of dried blood and mustard." You see the green satin sofa that "looks like slime on stagnant water." You hear the words echoing in the room of the Ritz-Carlton when Williams is told that his *Battle of Angels* must close at the end of its Boston run.

There is no arrogance here, however, to compound the essence of one's agony. Tennessee Williams is a writer, a distiller of the complexities of human nature—human nature which at one moment may be as delicate as a Japanese haiku and the next moment as brutal as a mother helplessly having to watch the murder of her child. This, to Williams, is just part of the realism/idealism dichotomy. A rose continues to smell softly sweet even as its thorns prick your fingers or as you strip the blossoms from the bush. In Williams's essays as in his plays, there is a tenderness toward humanity, a sympathy for human frustrations that, perhaps, can result only from a personal understanding of human weaknesses.

In addition, there is a freedom of both form and content in these essays not available to the artist in any other medium— in essence, Tennessee Williams interviews himself (as he actually does in "The World I Live In"). There is no interfering third party to distract from his statements or to inject an intervening perspective to his remarks.

The essays in this collection span a time period from 1944 through 1978. They are arranged in chronological order so that the reader can study the author's style, his changing awareness of the world around him, and the development of his aesthetic philosophy. In this way, too, the reader is invited to observe any parallel patterns in Williams's dramatic works.

Written over a long period of time, these essays were framed to suit a variety of purposes. For instance, "Questions Without Answers," like several others, was published in a newspaper in conjunction with the opening of a play. This, of course, poses a problem, as Williams notes: "Writing an article about your play prior to its New York opening is not going to improve the quality of the play, and moreover, it may have the disadvantage of suggesting to the suspicious that an effort is being made to load the dice." "Too Personal?" was composed to be included with the published version of *Small Craft Warnings;* "The Human Psyche—Alone" was a review of *The Delicate Prey and Other Stories,* a short story collection by Paul Bowles; "Biography of Carson McCullers" accompanied a book review in the *Saturday Review of Literature;* "Five Fiery Ladies" was a tribute to leading actresses who had appeared in one of Williams's plays either on stage or screen; "Facts About Me" was written for the album cover of a recording of excerpts from his poetry and plays; "Introduction to Carson McCullers's *Reflections in a Golden Eye*" was just that, and "If the Writing Is Honest" served as a preface to William Inge's *The Dark at the Top of the Stairs;* "Critic Says 'Evasion,' Writer Says 'Mystery'" and "Tennessee Williams Presents His POV" were written in response to critics' comments, the latter in answer to the charge that Williams and others have "chosen to explore the snake pits"; "Homage to Key West" and "The Pleasures of the Table" reveal a Tennessee Williams relaxed and away, however briefly, from his writing.

All of these essays are an exploration of the artistic possibilities and limitations of the theater, of the body, of the spirit, and of the human condition; each possesses a special charm as well as an undercurrent of humor and tenderness. In them, Tennessee Williams exposes a lyricism—a personal lyricism—not possible on the stage or through any other medium.

CHRISTINE R. DAY
DEARBORN, MICHIGAN

Acknowledgments

As is always the case with projects of this nature, it is impossible to list all of those people who have helped in many different ways. Particular appreciation should be acknowledged to Mr. James Laughlin of New Directions; Dr. Milton Foster, Head of the Department of English and American Literature, Eastern Michigan University; Dr. George Perkins, Professor, Department of English and American Literature, Eastern Michigan University; Beverly Dixon Schraufnagel; parents; family; and special friends.

C. R. D.

Preface to My Poems

FRIVOLOUS VERSION

I BEGAN WRITING verse at about the time of puberty, and one of my earliest lyrics is still the one recited most frequently at parties. It was an apostrophe to death, and I think it deserves to be quoted here because of its distinctive character and evidence of influences. The sextet follows:

> Rudely you seized and broke proud Sappho's lyre,
> Barret and Wylie went your songless way.
> You do not care what hecatomb of fire
> is split when shattering the urn of clay.
> Yet, Death, I'll pardon all you took away
> while still you spare me—glorious Millay!

Having disposed of women poets in this cavalier manner, I took the field with great audacity from the very beginning. I

This essay appeared in *Five Young American Poets,* Third Series, New Directions, 1944.

was quite successful, my poetry was much admired in high school and I won not only plaudits but many little prizes from women's clubs and poetry groups in Mississippi and Missouri. I remember when an officer in my mother's chapter of the DAR passed away, I composed an elegy to her which was read aloud at the services and resulted in a very moving catharsis. Poetry was my undoing, however, for when I left school and had employment in the warehouse of a wholesale shoe corporation, I formed the habit of retiring to a closet of the lavatory and spending unconscionably long periods of time working out rhyme schemes. When such unbusinesslike practices were exposed to the boss, I was slated for early dismissal and have never regained any standing in the commercial world for more than a few weeks' time.

Coeval with these early efforts, I became a friend of Clark Mills who lived in the town of Clayton, Mo., to which we had moved. Clark's admiration for my verse was tempered by a more technical approach than my other admirers'. He was usually given to owlish nods and bronchial noises when I showed him my verse. However, he did admire my plays and stories, and we subsequently formed what we called a "literary factory" in the basement of his suburban home. Ideas from Clark's verse went into my plays, and ideas from my plays went into Clark's verse, and it was a very creative and delightful arrangement, especially since Clark's mother visited us more regularly than the muse with trays of lemonade and sandwiches, and Clark usually had a bottle of wine stashed behind the shelves of poetry. It was Clark who warned me of the existence of people like Hart Crane and Rimbaud and Rilke, and my deep and sustained admiration for Clark's writing gently but firmly removed my attention from the more obvious to the purer voices in poetry. About this time I acquired my copy of Hart Crane's collected poems which I began to read with gradual comprehension.

The poems included in this volume are a sort of spiritual witness of these years: at least they are the product of an un-attached and nomadic existence of six or eight years' duration.

For me there was the dramatic intercession of Broadway, which I regard as fortuitous and beside the point since a poet who happens to stumble into the theater is not a case in point. I found good angels such as Audrey Wood, Margo Jones and the Rockefeller Foundation and some relatively altruistic pro-ducers such as the Group Theatre and the Theatre Guild to throw me a lifeline when I had reached the very last moment of endurance.

And today I received a telegram which will take me to Hollywood.

For others, I know, the Army has offered a haven. And they are actually more fortunate, I believe, than the so many more who were too battered and knocked about already to pass the physical and psychological examinations that candi-dates for extinction in the war are subjected to.

And so I propose the question: *How do we live?*

I can't think of anything more important to say.

SERIOUS VERSION

If there is ever a world congress of poets, I mean outside the one obliquely described in the section called *Walpurgis-*

nacht in Joyce's *Ulysses,* I think the problem mainly to be considered is not competitive philosophies of art nor even political ideas. Despite the fuss which many of us make over the latter and its indisputable importance, I think it always remains a little outside our introverted orbit. As for the first, it is altogether a matter of personal feeling and most of the arguments have worn themselves out. I think the problem that we should apply ourselves to is simply one of survival. I mean actual physical survival!

Whenever I meet a young poet, barring such eclectic examples as Charles Henri Ford and Jesse Stuart, for opposite reasons, I always involuntarily ask them: *How do you live? How do you get along?* just as a callously inquisitive visitor at a sideshow would ask the armless man how he unzipped his trousers.

I think it is almost impossible for a young poet to live in contemporary America, let alone contemporary Europe and Asia, and the fact that some of them do is far more surprising than the fact that so many *don't.*

The most destructible element in our society, the immature and rootless artists or poets, is the one that is subjected to the worst lambasting.

I know this, because I have survived it myself, and how I have survived is a question I ask myself with the same incredulous wonder that I have asked others such as—there are too many to name!

I haven't known them merely in New York, where poets know each other, but in New Orleans and in Los Angeles and in St. Louis and Chicago, all the big cities where groups of them huddle together for some dim, communal comfort—I have been a part of their groups because of the desperate necessity for the companionship of one's own kind, and I remember distinctly such people as Irene who painted the most powerful primitive canvases I've ever seen and whispered through shutters to men who passed on the street because she had a body that had to live. I remember Joe Turner who wrote sea stories, often as vivid and beautiful as Conrad's. He was a merchant sailor because there was nothing else for him to do when the W.P.A. Writers' Project ceased to exist, and now not only Joe but his mss. have disappeared altogether. And even those who were known and recognized, whose talents were given the slow and grudging appraisal of those who have the power to help young artists—I have known even those sparingly elected to find the struggle too complex and exhausting to go on with.

Hart Crane wasn't the only one.

I have lived in the middle of it since I was released from the comparative cocoon of schools and colleges and took to the road because the alternative was something too dull to endure.

About this time I also left Clayton, Mo., and took to moving about the country. During this nomadic period I began to write the poems which are included in this volume and a great many more, none of which left my hands before the present time, because I had no reliable mailing address. Oh, I did make one submission to a magazine of verse in Chicago. It was returned to me with a sharply worded complaint about the omission of return postage and it was signed "G.D.," which I assume were the initials of the editor and not anything more profane!

All at once some plays I had left in New York received

the spectacular and simultaneous attention of the Rockefeller Foundation, the Group Theatre, the Theatre Guild, and Audrey Wood. I was awarded a fellowship and drafted into the startling world of Broadway from which I have never altogether emerged, although I continue to knock about the country.

Symbolically I found a lot of books inconvenient to carry with me and gradually they dropped along the way—till finally there was only one volume with me, the book of Hart Crane.

I have it with me today, my only library and all of it. This does not mean a snobbish or hysterical exclusion of interest in other poets. On the contrary, I think my taste is unusually catholic, for I still enjoy all of the lady poets so briskly disposed of in the first sonnet. Wherever there is a truthful intensity of feeling, I like it—whether it's in Keats or Auden or even in the presently outlawed Mr. Pound, whom I heard over the short-wave from an Axis capital lately.

But I am inclined to value Crane a little above Eliot or anyone else because of his organic purity and sheer breathtaking power. I feel that he stands with Keats and Shakespeare and Whitman. Why argue about it? It's too personal a feeling.

If there is ever indeed a world congress of poets, I think the thing to fuss over is simply this: a method of survival! I mean actual, physical survival!

I think that we are going to have a hard time of it!

"Something Wild..."

WHILE I WAS on the road with *Summer and Smoke* I was
entertained one evening by the company of a successful community theater, one of the pioneer outfits of this kind and one
of the few that operate on a profitable self-supporting basis. It
had been ten years since I had had a connection with a community theater. I was professionally spawned by one ten years
ago in St. Louis, but like most offspring, once I departed from
the maternal shelter, I gave it scarcely a backward glance.
Backward glances are a bit impractical, anyhow, in a theatrical
career.

Now I felt considerable curiosity about the contact I was
about to renew: but the moment I walked in the door I felt
something wrong. Not so much something wrong as something
missing. It seemed all so respectable. The men in their conservative business suits with their neat haircuts and highly

This introduction for the Second Edition of 27 *Wagons Full of Cotton*,
New Directions, 1949, first appeared in the *New York Star* in 1945.

polished shoes could have passed for corporation lawyers and the women, mostly their wives, were impeccably ladylike. There was no scratchy phonograph music, there were no dimly lit alcoves where dancing couples stood practically still, no sofas with ruptured upholstery, no garlands of colored crepe paper festooning the ceiling and collapsing onto the floor.

In my opinion art is a kind of anarchy, and the theater is a province of art. What was missing here, was something an-archistic in the air. I must modify that statement about art and anarchy. Art is only anarchy in juxtaposition with or-ganized society. It runs counter to the sort of orderliness on which organized society apparently must be based. It is a be-nevolent anarchy: it must be that and if it is true art, it is. It is benevolent in the sense of constructing something which is missing, and what it constructs may be merely criticism of things as they exist. I felt in this group no criticism but rather an adaptation which was almost obsequious. And my mind shot back to the St. Louis group I have mentioned, a group called The Mummers.

The Mummers were sort of a long-haired outfit. Now there is no virtue, *per se*, in not going to the barber. And I don't suppose there is any particular virtue in girls having runs in their stockings. Yet one feels a kind of nostalgia for that sort of disorderliness now and then.

Somehow you associate it with things that have no logi-cal connection with it. You associate it with really good times and with intense feelings and with convictions. Most of all with convictions! In the party I have mentioned there was a notable lack of convictions. Nobody was shouting for—or against—anything, there was just a lot of polite chitchat going on among people who seemed to have known each other long enough to have exhausted all interest in each other's ideas.

While I stood there among them, the sense that something was missing clarified itself into a tremendous wave of longing for something that I had not been conscious of wanting until that moment. The open sky of my youth!—a peculiarly American youth which somehow seems to have slipped a little bit out of our grasp nowadays. . . .

The Mummers of St. Louis were my professional youth. They were the disorderly theater group of St. Louis, standing socially, if not also artistically, opposite to the usual Little Theater group. That opposite group need not be described. They were eminently respectable, predominantly middle-aged, and devoted mainly to the presentation of Broadway hits a season or two after Broadway. Their stage was narrow and notices usually mentioned how well they had overcome their spatial limitations, but it never seemed to me that they produced anything in a manner that needed to overcome limitations of space. The dynamism which is theater was as foreign to their philosophy as the tongue of Chinese.

Dynamism was what The Mummers had, and for about five years—roughly from about 1935 to 1940—they burned like one of Miss Millay's improvident little candles—and then expired. Yes, there was about them that kind of excessive romanticism which is youth and which is the best and purest part of life.

The first time I worked with them was in 1936, when I was a student at Washington University in St. Louis. They were, then, under the leadership of a man named Willard Holland, their organizer and their director. Holland always wore a blue suit which was not only baggy but shiny. He needed a haircut and he sometimes wore a scarf instead of a shirt. This was not what made him a great director, but a great director he was. Everything that he touched he charged with electricity. Was it my youth that made it seem that way? Possibly, but not probably. In fact not even possibly: you judge theater, really, by its effect on audiences, and Holland's work never failed to deliver, and when I say deliver I mean a sock!

The first thing I worked with them on was *Bury the Dead*, by Irwin Shaw. That play ran a little bit short of full length and they needed a curtain raiser to fill out the program. Holland called me up. He did not have a prepossessing voice. It was high-pitched and nervous. He said I hear you go to college and I hear you can write. I admitted some justice in both of these charges. Then he asked me: How do you feel about compulsory military training? I then assured him that I had left the University of Missouri because I could not get a passing grade in the ROTC. Swell! said Holland, you are just the guy I am looking for. How would you like to write something against militarism?

So I did.

Shaw's play, one of the greatest lyric plays America has produced, was a solid piece of flame. Actors and script, under Holland's dynamic hand, were one piece of vibrant living tissue. Now St. Louis is not a town that is easily impressed. They love music, they are ardent devotees of the symphony concerts, but they preserve a fairly rigid decorum when they are confronted with anything offbeat which they are not used to. They certainly were not used to the sort of hot lead which The Mummers pumped into their bellies that night of Shaw's play. They were not used to it, but it paralyzed them. There wasn't a cough or creak in the house, and nobody left the Wednesday Club Auditorium (which The Mummers rented out for their performances) without a disturbing kink in their nerves or guts, and I doubt if any of them have forgotten it to this day.

It was The Mummers that I remembered at this polite supper party which I attended last month.

Now let me give you a picture of The Mummers! Most of them worked at other jobs besides theater. They had to, because The Mummers were not a paying proposition. There were laborers. There were clerks. There were waitresses. There were students. There were whores and tramps and there was even a post-debutante who was a member of the Junior League of St. Louis. Many of them were fine actors. Many of them were not. Some of them could not act at all, but what they lacked in ability, Holland inspired them with in the way of enthusiasm. I guess it was all run by a kind of beautiful witchcraft! It was like a definition of what I think theater is. Something wild, something exciting, something that you are not used to. Offbeat is the word.

They put on bad shows sometimes, but they never put on a show that didn't deliver a punch to the solar plexus, maybe not in the first act, maybe not in the second, but always at last a good hard punch was delivered, and it made a difference in the lives of the spectators that they had come to that place and seen that show.

The plays I gave them were bad. But the first of these plays was a smash hit. It even got rave notices out of all three papers, and there was a real demonstration on the opening night with shouts and cheers and stamping, and the pink-faced author took his first bow among the gray-faced coal miners that he had created out of an imagination never stimulated by the sight of an actual coal mine. The second play that I gave them, *Fugitive Kind,* was a flop. It got one rave notice out of the *Star-Times,* but the *Post-Dispatch* and the *Globe Democrat* gave it hell. Nevertheless it packed a considerable wallop and there are people in St. Louis who still remember it. Bad plays, both of them, amateurish and coarse and juvenile and talky. But Holland and his players put them across the footlights without apology and they put them across with the bang that is theater.

Oh, how long ago that was!

The Mummers lived only five years. Yes, they had something in common with lyric verse of too romantic nature. From 1935 to 1940 they had their fierce little flame, and then they expired, and now there is not a visible trace of them. Where is Holland? In Hollywood, I think. And where are the players? God knows. . . .

I am here, remembering them wistfully.

Now I shall have to say something to give this recollection a meaning to you.

All right. This is it.

Today we are living in a world which is threatened by totalitarianism. The Fascist and the Communist states have thrown us into a panic of reaction. Reactionary opinion descends like a ton of bricks on the head of any artist who speaks out against the current of prescribed ideas. We are all under wraps of one kind or another, trembling before the specter of investigating committees and even with Buchenwald in the back of our minds when we consider whether or not we dare to say we were for Henry Wallace. *Yes, it is as bad as that.*

And yet it isn't *really* as bad as that.

America is still America, democracy is still democracy.

In our history books are still the names of Jefferson and Lincoln and Tom Paine. The direction of the democratic impulse, which is entirely and irresistibly away from the police state and away from any and all forms of controlled thought and feeling—which is entirely and irresistibly in the direction of that which is individual and humane and equitable and free—that direction can be confused but it cannot be lost.

I have a way of jumping from the particular to the abstract, for the particular is sometimes as much as we know of the abstract.

Now let me jump back again: where? To the subject of community theaters and their social function.

It seems to me, as it seems to many artists right now, that an effort is being made to put creative work and workers under wraps.

Nothing could be more dangerous to Democracy, for the irritating grain of sand which is creative work in a society must be kept inside the shell or the pearl of idealistic progress cannot be made. For God's sake let us defend ourselves against whatever is hostile to us without imitating the thing which we are afraid of!

Community theaters have a social function and it is to be that kind of an irritant in the shell of their community.

Not to conform, not to wear the conservative business suit of their audience, but to let their hair grow long and even greasy, to make wild gestures, break glasses, fight, shout, and fall downstairs! When you see them acting like this—not respectably, not quite decently, even!—then you will know that something is going to happen in that outfit, something disturbing, something irregular, something brave and honest.

The biologist will tell you that progress is the result of mutations. Mutations is another word for freaks. For God's sake let's have a little more freakish behavior—not less.

Maybe ninety per cent of the freaks will be just freaks, ludicrous and pathetic and getting nowhere but into trouble.

Eliminate them, however—bully them into conformity—and nobody in America will ever be really young any more and we'll be left standing in the dead center of nowhere.

On a
Streetcar Named Success

THIS WINTER MARKED the third anniversary of the Chicago opening of *The Glass Menagerie,* an event which terminated one part of my life and began another about as different in all external circumstances as could well be imagined. I was snatched out of virtual oblivion and thrust into sudden prominence, and from the precarious tenancy of furnished rooms about the country I was removed to a suite in a first-class Manhattan hotel. My experience was not unique. Success has often come that abruptly into the lives of Americans. The Cinderella story is our favorite national myth, the cornerstone of the film industry if not of the Democracy itself. I have seen it enacted on the screen so often that I am now inclined to yawn at it, not with disbelief but with an attitude of Who

---

A version of this essay first appeared in the *New York Times,* November 30, 1947, four days before the opening of *A Streetcar Named Desire.* Another version of this same essay, titled "The Catastrophe of Success" is sometimes used as an introduction to *The Glass Menagerie.*

Cares! Anyone with such beautiful teeth and hair as the screen protagonist of such a story was bound to have a good time one way or another, and you could bet your bottom dollar and all the tea in China that that one would not be caught dead or alive at any meeting involving a social conscience.

No, my experience was not exceptional, but neither was it quite ordinary, and if you are willing to accept the somewhat eclectic proposition that I had not been writing with such an experience in mind—and many people are not willing to believe that a playwright is interested in anything but popular success—there may be some point in comparing the two estates.

The sort of life which I had had previous to this popular success was one that required endurance, a life of clawing and scratching along a sheer surface and holding on tight with raw fingers to every inch of rock higher than the one caught hold of before, but it was a good life because it was the sort of life for which the human organism is created.

I was not aware of how much vital energy had gone into this struggle until the struggle was removed. I was out on a level plateau with my arm still thrashing and my lungs still grabbing at air that no longer resisted. This was security at last.

I sat down and looked about me and was suddenly very depressed. I thought to myself, this is just a period of adjustment. Tomorrow morning I will wake up in this first-class hotel suite above the discreet hum of an East Side boulevard and I will appreciate its elegance and luxuriate in its comforts and know that I have arrived at our American plan of Olympus. Tomorrow morning when I look at the green satin sofa I will fall in love with it. It is only temporarily that the green satin looks like slime on stagnant water.

But in the morning the inoffensive little sofa looked more revolting than the night before, and I was already getting too fat for the $125 suit which a fashionable acquaintance had selected for me. In the suite things began to break accidentally. An arm came off the sofa. Cigarette burns appeared on the polished surface of the furniture. Windows were left open and a rainstorm flooded the suite. But the maid always put it straight and the patience of the management was inexhaustible. Late parties could not offend them seriously. Nothing short of a demoltion bomb seemed to bother my neighbors.

I lived on room service. But in this, too, there was a disenchantment. Some time between the moment when I ordered dinner over the phone and when it was rolled into my living room like a corpse on a rubber-wheeled table, I lost all interest in it. Once I ordered a sirloin steak and a chocolate sundae, but everything was so cunningly disguised on the table that I mistook the chocolate sauce for gravy and poured it over the sirloin steak.

Of course all this was the more trivial aspect of a spiritual dislocation that began to manifest itself in far more disturbing ways. I soon found myself becoming indifferent to people. A well of cynicism rose in me. Conversations all sounded as if they had been recorded years ago and were being played back on a turntable. Sincerity and kindliness seemed to have gone out of my friends' voices. I suspected them of hypocrisy. I stopped calling them, stopped seeing them. I was impatient of what I took to be inane flattery.

[17]

I got so sick of hearing people say, "I loved your play!" that I could not say thank you any more. I choked on the words and turned rudely away from the usually sincere person. I no longer felt any pride in the play itself but began to dislike it, probably because I felt too lifeless inside ever to create another. I was walking around dead in my shoes and I knew it but there were no friends I knew or trusted sufficiently, at that time, to take them aside and tell them what was the matter.

This curious condition persisted about three months, till late spring, when I decided to have another eye operation mainly because of the excuse it gave me to withdraw from the world behind a gauze mask. It was my fourth eye operation, and perhaps I should explain that I had been afflicted for about five years with a cataract on my left eye which required a series of needling operations and finally an operation on the muscle of the eye. (The eye is still in my head. So much for that.)

Well, the gauze mask served a purpose. While I was resting in the hospital the friends whom I had neglected or affronted in one way or another began to call on me, and now that I was in pain and darkness, their voices seemed to have changed, or rather that unpleasant mutation which I had suspected earlier in the season had now disappeared and they sounded now as they had used to sound in the lamented days of my obscurity. Once more they were sincere and kindly voices with the ring of truth in them and that quality of understanding for which I had originally sought them out.

As far as my physical vision was concerned, this last operation was only relatively successful (although it left me with an apparently clear black pupil in the right position, or nearly so) but in another, figurative way, it had served a much deeper purpose.

When the gauze mask was removed I found myself in a readjusted world. I checked out of the handsome suite at the first-class hotel, packed my papers and a few incidental belongings, and left for Mexico, an elemental country where you can quickly forget the false dignities and conceits imposed by success, a country where vagrants innocent as children curl up to sleep on the pavements and human voices, especially when their language is not familiar to the ear, are soft as birds'. My public self, that artifice of mirrors, did not exist here and so my natural being was resumed.

Then, as a final act of restoration, I settled for a while at Chapala to work on a play called *The Poker Night,* which later became *A Streetcar Named Desire.* It is only in his work that an artist can find reality and satisfaction, for the actual world is less intense than the world of his invention, and consequently his life, without recourse to violent disorder, does not seem very substantial. The right condition for him is that in which his work is not only convenient but unavoidable.

For me a convenient place to work is a remote place among strangers where there is good swimming. But life should require a certain minimal effort. You should not have too many people waiting on you; you should have to do most things for yourself. Hotel service is embarrassing. Maids, waiters, bellhops, porters, and so forth are the most embarrassing people in the world for they continually remind you of inequities which we accept as the proper thing. The sight of an ancient woman, gasping and wheezing as she drags a heavy pail of water down a hotel corridor to mop up the mess of some drunken overprivileged guest, is one that sickens and weighs upon the heart and withers it with shame for this world in which it is not only tolerated but regarded as proof positive that the wheels of Democracy are functioning as they should without interference from above or below. Nobody should have to clean up anybody else's mess in this world. It is terribly bad for both parties, but probably worse for the one receiving the service.

I have been corrupted as much as anyone else by the vast number of menial services which our society has grown to expect and depend on. We should do for ourselves or let the machines do for us—the glorious technology that is supposed to be the new light of the world. We are like a man who has bought a great amount of equipment for a camping trip, who has the canoe and the tent and the fishing lines and the axe and the guns, the mackinaw and the blankets, but who now, when all the preparations and the provisions are piled expertly together, is suddenly too timid to set out on the journey but remains where he was yesterday and the day before and day before that, looking suspiciously through white lace curtains at the clear sky he distrusts. Our great technology is a God-given chance for adventure and for progress which we are afraid to attempt. Our ideas and our ideals remain exactly what they were and where they were three centuries ago. No. I beg your pardon. It is no longer safe for a man to even declare them!

This is a long excursion from a small theme into a large one which I did not intend to make, so let me go back to what I was saying before.

[20]

This is an oversimplification. One does not escape that easily from the seduction of an effete way of life. You cannot arbitrarily say to yourself, I will now continue my life as it was before this thing, Success, happened to me. But once you fully apprehend the vacuity of a life without struggle you are equipped with the basic means of salvation. Once you know this is true, that the heart of man, his body and his brain, are forged in a white-hot furnace for the purpose of conflict (the struggle of creation) and that with the conflict removed, the man is a sword cutting daisies, that not privation but luxury is the wolf at the door and that the fangs of this wolf are all the little vanities and conceits and laxities that Success is heir to—why, then with this knowledge you are at least in a position of knowing where danger lies.

You know, then, that the public Somebody you are when you "have a name" is a fiction created with mirrors and that the only somebody worth being is the solitary and unseen you that existed from your first breath and which is the sum of your actions and so is constantly in a state of becoming under your own volition—and knowing these things, you can even survive the catastrophe of Success!

It is never altogether too late, unless you embrace the Bitch Goddess, as William James called her, with both arms and find in her smothering caresses exactly what the home-sick little boy in you always wanted, absolute protection and utter effortlessness. Security is a kind of death, I think, and it can come to you in a storm of royalty checks beside a kidney-shaped pool in Beverly Hills or anywhere at all that is re-moved from the conditions that made you an artist, if that's what you are or were or intended to be. Ask anyone who has experienced the kind of success I am talking about—What good is it? Perhaps to get an honest answer you will have to give him a shot of truth serum but the word he will finally groan is unprintable in genteel publications.

Then what is good? The obsessive interest in human affairs, plus a certain amount of compassion and moral conviction, that first made the experience of living something that must be translated into pigment or music or bodily movement or poetry or prose or anything that's dynamic and expressive—that's what's good for you if you're at all serious in your aims. William Saroyan wrote a great play on this theme, that purity of heart is the one success worth having. "In the time of your life—live!" That time is short and it doesn't return again. It is slipping away while I write this and while you read it, and the monosyllable of the clock is Loss, loss, loss, unless you devote your heart to its opposition.

Questions Without Answers

WRITING AN ARTICLE about your play prior to its New York opening is not going to improve the quality of the play and, moreover, it may have the disadvantage of suggesting to the suspicious that an effort is being made to load the dice.

It is possible, though I prefer to think unlikely, that no ethical consideration would deter me from making this effort if I thought it likely to pay off, and God knows pretension has been known to pay off in some branches of the arts. Inflated reputations and eclectic styles have cast an aura of gravity over much that is essentially vacuous in painting; obscurity has disguised sterility in a good deal of verse.

But the theater, which is called the charlatan of the arts, is paradoxically the one in which the charlatan is most easily detected. He must say intelligibly what he has to say and unless it is well worth saying he does not have a Chinaman's chance of surviving. Even cheap entertainment is honest. It

This essay first appeared in the *New York Times*, October 3, 1948.

is all honest that does what it professes to do, and there is too much hot light and too many penetrating eyes cast upon the stage for the willful obscurantist to pull his tricks.

But writing an article about your play puts you in a fairly untenable position. Three courses seem to be open. You can praise it or you can denigrate it or you can explain it. The first is surely fatal, although it has been attempted. The second is foolish. If you sincerely thought it was a bad play you would not have put it into production, because the failure of a play is one of the world's more agonizing adventures. To explain is okay if there is something that needs explaining.

Obviously, I have already chosen the third one of these three alternatives. The problem now is to find something in my work which needs explaining.

I have been asked a lot of questions about my plays. Recently, only last week, the cast of *Summer and Smoke* was entertained at a supper given by Lester and Cleo Gruber at a suburb in Detroit. Everything was wonderful: it was the first good time we had all had together on the road and it was wonderfully relaxing after the tension of two openings and some highly charged atmosphere in suites at the Statler and the Book-Cadillac.

Earlier in the evening the party was conducted in the rathskeller of this suburban residence. With our backs to the rathskeller bar, behind which stood a white-jacketed youth passing out drinks as fast as an elbow can bend, the director, Margo Jones, and myself withstood a barrage of questions like a pair of antlered beasts, and withstood them successfully. But it was now later in the evening, the rathskeller bar had shut down and the party had progressed, if progression you call it, from cocktails and highballs to cole slaw and beef tongue.

That comfortable stupefaction which belongs to the late hours of Sunday had fallen over me and I had retreated with a plate of food to an alcove in the parlor. This alcove was something of a cul-de-sac. It had a fine view but no exit, and if you've seen or read Sartre you know how discomfiting no exit can be, especially when there get to be women in it. That was what happened.

A fresh contingent of visitors arrived at the Gruber residence and headed straight for this alcove. All at once I found myself hemmed in by three women in basic black who had been to the Saturday matinee and had apparently thought of nothing since except the problems of Alma Winemiller, the heroine of *Summer and Smoke*. When you are eating, a great deal can be accomplished by having a mouth full of food and by making guttural noises instead of speech when confronted with questions such as, What is the theme of your play? What happens to the characters after the play is over? Why do you write? What is your next play about and how do you happen to know so much about women? On that last one you can spit the food out if it really begins to choke you!

For a writer who is not intentionally obscure, and never, in his opinion, obscure at all, I do get asked a hell of a lot of questions which I can't answer. I have never been able to say what was the theme of my play and I don't think I have ever been conscious of writing with a theme in mind. I am always surprised when, after a play has opened, I read in the papers what the play is about, that it was about a decayed Southern belle trying to get a man for her crippled daughter, or that it was about a boozy floozy on the skids, or a backwoods sheik in a losing battle with three village vamps.

Don't misunderstand me. I am thankful for these highly condensed and stimulating analyses, but it would never have occurred to me that that was the story I was trying to tell. Usually when asked about a theme, I look vague and say, "It is a play about life." What could be simpler, and yet more pretentious? You can easily extend that a little and say it is a tragedy of incomprehension. That also means life. Or you can say it is a tragedy of Puritanism. That is life in America. Or you can say it is a play that considers the "problem of evil." But why not just say "life"?

To return to the women in the alcove. On this particular occasion the question that floored me was "Why do you always write about frustrated women?"

To say that floored me is to put it mildly, because I would say that frustrated is almost exactly what the women I write about are not. What was frustrated about Amanda Wingfield? Circumstances, yes! But spirit? See Helen Hayes in London's *The Glass Menagerie* if you still think Amanda was a frustrated spirit! No, there is nothing interesting about frustration *per se*. I could not write a line about it for the simple reason that I can't write a line about anything that bores me.

Was Blanche of *A Streetcar Named Desire* frustrated? About as frustrated as a beast of the jungle! And Alma Winemiller? What is frustrated about loving with such white-hot intensity that it alters the whole direction of your life, and removes you from the parlor of an Episcopal rectory to a secret room above Moon Lake Casino?

[26]

I did not have to answer the lady who asked me this question. Into the fiery breach jumped—Margo Jones!

"Tennessee does not write about frustrated women!" she shouted. "Tennessee does not write about abnormal characters!"

She had arrived at the alcove and was making an entrance.

"Oh?" said one of the ladies. "Then what does he write about?"

"People!" said Margo. "Life."

"Now, honey," she continued, in a less militant tone, "I don't know a thing about you women, but just looking at you, I can see you have problems!"

By this time I had executed a flanking movement under the cover of Margo's diversionary tactics. The alcove, the women, the questions and finally even the residence were behind me and I stood on the suburban sidewalk, still with a plate of food and no work but ten fingers, and I suddenly felt very happy, not that I had escaped from the questions but that there were people who cared enough to ask them.

The mysterious thing about writing plays about life is that so many people find them so strange and baffling. That makes you know, with moments of deep satisfaction, that you have really succeeded in writing about it!

A Writer's Quest
for a Parnassus

Rome

AMONG THE MANY misapprehensions held about writers is the idea that they follow a peaceful profession, an idea that derives from the fact that most writers have a sedentary appearance and that most writing is done in a more or less stationary position, usually seated in a chair at a table. But writing is actually a violent activity. It is actually more violent than any other profession that I can think of, including that of the professional wrestler. And writers, when they are not writing, must find some outer violence that is equivalent, or nearly, to the inner one they are used to. They find it difficult to remain long in one place, for writing books and taking voyages are corresponding gestures.

If the writer is truly a writer and not someone who has adopted the vocation as a convenient social pose to excuse his predilection for various kinds of waywardness, his first concern, when he goes traveling, will be to discover that magic

This essay appeared in the *New York Times Magazine,* August 13, 1950.

[28]

place of all places where the work goes better than it has gone before, the way that a gasoline motor picks up when you switch it from regular to high octane. For one of the mysterious things about writing is the extreme susceptibility it shows to the influence of places. Almost every writer has a certain place that he associates, perhaps through mere superstition, with his periods of greatest fertility. But sooner or later this particular place will be exhausted for him and he must find ⟨3⟩ another.

Often this quest will take him out of America. Often it will take him back to America if he has left there. The interval of seeking may be a long one. It may be six months or a year, or the years may be several, but eventually he will find the new place that looks and feels and smells mysteriously like home, and then he will turn around two or three times in his tracks, the way a dog does, sniffing the air in all directions before he sets himself down for the period of outer oblivion and inner violence that his work demands of him.

British and American writers are more inclined to travel than others. I think the British travel to get out of the rain, but the American artist travels for a more particular reason, and for one that I hesitate to mention lest I be summoned before some investigating committee in Congress. Putting that hesitation at least partially aside, let me venture the suggestion that America is no longer a terribly romantic part of the world, and that writers, all except, possibly, Upton Sinclair and Sinclair Lewis, are essentially romantic spirits— or they would not be writing.

Now there are only two cities left in America with a romantic appeal, however vestigial, and they are, of course, New

Orleans and San Francisco. Our industrial dynamism has dispelled whatever magic the other great cities may once have possessed. Occasionally an artist may attempt to create a poetic synthesis out of this very dynamism of ours. Hart Crane attempted it, and, in my opinion, he succeeded in it. But one may take warning from the fact that, in spite of his achievement, he jumped off a boat returning to New York from a romantic retreat into Mexico.

Among writers' places there has always been Paris. If you remember the early histories of Hemingway, Fitzgerald, Westcott, Stein and so on, you may well have the impression that Paris offers great stimulation to the expatriate American writers. Well, it no longer does. Paris itself has not changed, it is still the most spacious and elegant capital of the world, and there is now a definite upswing of creative activity among the native French: Jean-Paul Sartre and Albert Camus, for instance. But the effect on young Americans who go there, ostensibly, to write their first books, is one that appears to be vitiating.

You find these new expatriate writers mostly about the Left Bank district known as St. Germain-des-Prés, sitting on the sidewalk in front of the Café de Flore or the Deux Maggots or the Reine Blanche, according to their degree of Bohemianism. And they sit there, literally, from dusk until dawn. At daybreak they disappear with each other into shabby little hotels. They go to bed drunk and they wake up hung over and usually in the company of someone they barely remember meeting who looks much worse in the light of noon than in the blur of an alcoholic dawn. It is mid-afternoon before the company has departed and the typewriter hauled from under the bed. The typewriter, of course, needs repairing. The machine is heavy and the repair shop is far, and presently the whole idea is abandoned and they have repaired, themselves, to the sidewalk tables.

The troublesome question, and the one I find it impossible to answer to my own satisfaction, is whether or not these rootless young people would be better off had they remained in America. Obviously they found something lacking at home, and surely they find something in Paris besides the shopworn sophistication of their café circuit. But, whatever it is that they find, it is not a healthy, sustaining center about which their young personalities can form. I did not realize this so keenly when I first knew them in the summer of 1948, but when I came back a year later, and then another year later, and found the same boys and girls sitting on the same sidewalks, circulating among the same changeless cafés, the attritions that they had undergone became starkly evident.

With little effort at cohesion, let's turn sharply south. In Rome there is only one street where people make a social practice of sitting on the sidewalk. That is Via Veneto. It seems, at times, to be given over almost entirely to Americans and streetwalkers and boys picking up discarded cigarette butts. But it's a beautiful street. It winds like an old river among the great hotels and the American Embassy and the fashionable places for Americans to sit in the sun. To some Americans the sun of Rome is stupefying. To others it is merely tranquilizing. To both it is an escape from the feverish, high-pitched atmosphere of a typical urban society. To me Rome is far more beautiful than Paris. It is not a night city. In Rome there are only two resorts where an American

can sit up drinking all night, and I mention that fact because it is entirely relevant. It is what so many Americans seem to want to do in Europe. The two places where they can do it, in Rome, are the Jicky Club and the Caffè Notturno. Most of them go to the Jicky Club, which is on the Via Veneto, because it is more like our own American night-spots. The Caffè Notturno is quite another thing. It is where procurers and their ladies get together, about two or three in the morning to exchange their gossip of the Rialto.

Before I came to Rome I was concerned about the change I feared that the Holy Year might have produced in my favorite city of the world. But in Rome you will find no SRO sign. We came down by way of the Italian Alps and on the road we passed only one set of holy pilgrims. It was a cavalcade of motorcyclists from Holland, and it was headed by a young priest in his clerical garments. No doubt it was the strangest crossing of the Alps since Hannibal and his elephants. I had never before seen a priest on a motorcycle, and I must admit that he rode it with dignity and assurance and the look he gave us, as we whizzed past him, was one of grave friendliness.

Rome is actually less crowded than it was last summer. The Vatican has built a lot of new buildings especially for the housing of pilgrims, and that's where they seem to stay. You don't see them in the best restaurants or the interesting worldly places. Since I like to eat well and do not visit churches, I have not seen many of the pilgrims except on the road to Rome.

Rome and Italy cannot be all things to all people, but to me it is the place where I find the sun not only in the sky, where Italy also keeps it, but in the heart of the people. Before I came here for the first time, in the winter of 1948—with the fatigue of years suddenly fallen upon me—I had begun to think that a smile was something that people performed by a muscular contraction at the corners of their mouths. In a short while I found out that a smile can be something that happens between the heart and the eyes and that the muscular spasm about the mouth may be only the shadow of it.

Rome spells peace, which is what I want above all. But it spells it without isolation, which I don't want. I want to have peace in the middle of many people, and here I find it. And I can work here. That's the thing.

If it is not your city—perhaps you'd like Venice. I could not go to Venice, now, without hearing the haunted cadences of Hemingway's new novel. It is the saddest city, and when I say I think it is the best and most honest work that Hemingway has done, you may think me crazy. It will probably be a popular book. The critics may treat it pretty roughly. But its hauntingly tired cadences are the direct speech of a man's heart who is speaking that directly for the first time, and that makes it, for me, the finest thing Hemingway has done. But the city is sad, to me, as the memory of the deepest loss I could suffer. It seems to be built, the very gray stones of it and the green-gray water, out of a loss that is almost too bitter to still have poetry in it.

Perhaps you might find the Italian islands to be your place to write. You could go to Capri but it is too much of a picture postcard for my taste and it is the only place I know where the human male manages to outdress the female. Ischia has equally fine bathing at more accessible beaches

[33]

and the vacationers do not put on such highfalutin airs and outrageous plumage! W. H. Auden lives there, and if you're an American or British writer, you may have to apply to him for your visa.

I have not yet been to Sicily this year. Truman Capote has unfurled his Bronzini scarf above the fashionable resort of Taormina. He is supposedly in D. H. Lawrence's old house. Also there, I am told, is André Gide and the young American writer, Donald Windham, whose new novel *The Dog Star* contains the most sensitive new writing since Carson McCullers emerged ten years ago.

Regardless of where you may go in Europe this summer of 1950, you will find that places have a sadness under the surface. Everywhere the people seem to be waiting for the next cataclysm to strike them. They are not panicky, perhaps not even frightened, but they are waiting for it to happen with a feeling of fatality which you cannot help sensing unless you stay drunk the whole time or keep your nose in museums.

Nevertheless, the people want to survive, they want to keep on living through it, whatever it may be. Their history has made them wiser than Americans. It has also made them more tolerant, more patient, and considerably more human as well as a great deal sadder.

If these comments make me seem the opposite of a chauvinist, it is because of my honest feeling, after three years of foreign travel, that human brotherhood that stops at borders is not only delusive and foolish but enormously evil. The Marshall Plan must be translated, now, and amended, into spirit, if the dreaded thing that the Western World is waiting for can still be averted.

[34]

The Human Psyche — Alone

PAUL BOWLES IS a man and author of exceptional latitude but he has, like nearly all serious artists, a dominant theme. That theme is the fearful isolation of the individual being. He is as preoccupied with this isolation as the collectivist writers of ten years ago were concerned with group membership and purposes. Our contemporary American society seems no longer inclined to hold itself open to very explicit criticism from within. This is what we hope and suppose to be a transitory condition that began with the Second World War. It will probably wear itself out, for it is directly counter to the true American nature and tradition, but at the present time it seems to be entering its extreme phase, the all but complete suppression of any dissident voices. What choice has the artist, now, but withdrawal into the caverns of his own isolated being? Hence the outgrowth of the "new school of

This review of Paul Bowles's *The Delicate Prey and Other Stories* appeared in the *Saturday Review of Literature,* December 23, 1950.

decadence," so bitterly assailed by the same forces that turned our writers inward? Young men are writing first novels with a personal lyricism much like that exhibited in the early poems of the late Edna St. Vincent Millay, a comparison which is disparaging to neither party nor to the quality itself. For what is youth without lyricism, and what would lyricism be without a personal accent?

But Paul Bowles cannot be accurately classed with these other young men, not only because he is five or ten years older than most of them but because, primarily, a personal lyricism is not what distinguishes his work. His work is distinguished by its nature philosophical content, which is another thing altogether. As I noted in a review of his first novel, *The Sheltering Sky*, Bowles is apparently the only American writer whose work reflects the extreme spiritual dislocation (and a philosophical adjustment to it) of our immediate times. He has "an organic continuity" with the present in a way that is commensurate with the great French trio of Camus, Genet, and Sartre. This does little to improve his stock with the school of criticism which advocates a literature that is happily insensitive to any shock or abrasion, the sort that would sing "Hail, Hail, the Gang's all Here" while being extricated, still vocally alive, from the debris of a Long Island railroad disaster.

But to revert to the opening observation in this review, Paul Bowles is preoccupied with the spiritual isolation of individual beings. This is not a thing as simple as loneliness. Certainly a terrible kind of loneliness is expressed in most of these stories and in the novel that preceded them to publication, but the isolated beings in these stories have deliberately

chosen their isolation in most cases, not merely accepted and
endured it. There is a singular lack of human give-and-take,
of true emotional reciprocity, in the groups of beings assem-
bled upon his intensely but somberly lighted sets. The drama
is that of the single being rather than of beings in relation to
each other. Paul Bowles has experienced an unmistakable
revulsion from the act of social participation. One may sur-
mise in him the social experience of two decades. Then the
withdrawal is logical. The artist is not a man who will advance against a bayonet pressed to his abdomen unless another
bayonet is pressed to his back, and even then he is not likely
to move forward. He will, if possible, stand still. But Mr.
Bowles has discovered that the bayonet is pointed at the
man moving forward in our times, and that a retreat is still
accessible. He has done the sensible thing under these circumstances. He has gone back into the cavern of himself.
These seventeen stories are the exploration of a cavern of
individual sensibilities, and fortunately the cavern is a deep
one containing a great deal that is worth exploring.

Nowhere in any writing that I can think of has the sepa-
rateness of the one human psyche been depicted more vividly
and shockingly. If one feels that life achieves its highest
value and significance in those rare moments—they are
scarcely longer than that—when two lives are confluent, when
the walls of isolation momentarily collapse between two persons, and if one is willing to acknowledge the possibility of
such intervals, however rare and brief and difficult they may
be, the intensely isolated spirit evoked by Paul Bowles may
have an austerity which is frightening at least. But don't make
the mistake of assuming that what is frightening is necessarily

[37]

inhuman. It is curious to note that the spirit evoked by Bowles in so many of these stories does *not* seem inhuman, nor does it strike me as being antipathetic.

Even in the stories where this isolation is most shockingly, even savagely, stated and underlined the reader may sense an inverted kind of longing and tenderness for the thing whose absence the story concerns. This inverted, subtly implicit kind of tenderness comes out most clearly in one of the less impressive stories of the collection. This story is called "The Scorpion." It concerns an old woman in a primitive society of some obscure kind who has been left to live in a barren cave by her two sons. One of these deserters eventually returns to the cave with the purpose of bringing his mother to the community in which he and his brother have taken up residence. But the old woman is reluctant to leave her cave. The cave, too small for more than one person to occupy, is the only thing in reality that she trusts or feels at home in. It is curtained by rainfall and it is full of scorpions and it is not furnished by any kind of warmth or comfort, yet she would prefer to remain there than to accompany her son, who has finally, for some reason not stated in the story, decided to take her back with him to the community where he has moved. The journey must be made on foot and it will take three days. They finally set out together, but for the old woman there is no joy in the anticipation of a less isolated existence: there is only submission to a will that she does not interpret.

Here is a story that sentimentality, even a touch of it, could have destroyed. But sentimentality is a thing that you will find nowhere in the work of Paul Bowles. When he fails, which is rarely, it is for another reason. It is because now and then his special hardness of perception, his defiant rejection of all things emollient have led him into an area in which a man can talk only to himself.

The volume contains among several fine stories at least one that is a true masterpiece of short fiction—"A Distant Episode," published first in *Partisan Review*. In this story Paul Bowles states the same theme which he developed more fully in his later novel. The theme is the collapse of the civilized "Super Ego" into a state of almost mindless primitivism, totally dissociated from society except as an object of its unreasoning hostility. It is his extremely powerful handling of this theme again and again in his work which makes Paul Bowles probably the American writer who represents most truly the fierily and blindly explosive world that we live in so precariously from day and night to each uncertain tomorrow.

Introduction to
Carson McCullers's
Reflections in a Golden Eye

This book, *Reflections in a Golden Eye,* is a second novel, and although its appreciation has steadily risen during the years since its first appearance, it was then regarded as somewhat disappointing in the way that second novels usually are. When the book preceding a second novel has been very highly acclaimed, as was *The Heart Is a Lonely Hunter,* there is an inclination on the part of critics to retrench their favor, so nearly automatic and invariable a tendency that it can almost be set down as a physical law. But the reasons for failure to justly evaluate this second novel go beyond the common, temporal disadvantage that all second novels must suffer, and I feel that an examination of these reasons may be of considerably greater pertinence to our aim of suggesting a fresh evaluation.

To quote directly from book notices is virtually impossi-

This essay appeared as the introduction to Carson McCullers's *Reflections in a Golden Eye,* New Directions, 1950.

ble, here in Rome where I am writing these comments, but I believe that I am safe in assuming that it was their identification of the author with a certain school of American writers, mostly of Southern origin, that made her subject to a particular and powerful line of attack.

Even in the preceding book some readers must undoubtedly have detected a warning predisposition toward certain elements which are popularly known as "morbid." Doubtless there were some critics, as well as readers, who did not understand why Carson McCullers had elected to deal with a matter so unwholesome as the spiritual but passionate attachment that existed between a deaf-mute and a half-wit. But the tenderness of the book disarmed them. The depth and nobility of its compassion were so palpable that at least for the time being the charge of decadence had to be held in check. This forbearance was of short duration. In her second novel the veil of subjective tenderness, which is the one quality of her talent which she has occasionally used to some excess, was drawn away. And the young writer suddenly flashed in their faces the cabalistic emblems of fellowship with a certain company of writers that the righteous "Humanists" in the world of letters regarded as most abhorrent and most necessary to expose and attack.

Not being a follower of literary journals, I am not at all sure what title has been conferred upon this group of writers by their disparaging critics, but for my own convenience I will refer to them as the Gothic school. It has a very ancient lineage, this school, but our local inheritance of its tradition was first brought into prominence by the early novels of William Faulkner, who still remains a most notorious and

[41]

unregenerate member. There is something in the region, something in the blood and culture, of the Southern state that has somehow made them the center of this Gothic school of writers. Certainly something more important than the influence of a single artist, Faulkner, is to be credited with its development, just as in France the Existentialist movement is surely attributable to forces more significant than the personal influence of Jean-Paul Sartre. There is actually a common link between the two schools, French and American, but characteristically the motor impulse of the French school is intellectual and philosophic while that of the American is more of an emotional and romantic nature. What is this common link? In my opinion it is most simply definable as a sense, an intuition, of an underlying dreadfulness in modern experience.

The question one hears most frequently about writers of the Gothic school is this little classic:

"Why do they write about such *dreadful* things?"

This is a question that escapes not only from the astonished lips of summer matrons who have stumbled into the odd world of William Faulkner, through some inadvertence or mischief at the lending library, but almost as frequently and certainly more importantly, from the pens of some of the most eminent book critics. If it were a solely and typically philistine manifestation, there would be no sense or hope in trying to answer it, but the fact that it is used as a major line of attack by elements that the artist has to deal with—critics, publishers, distributors, not to mention the reading public—makes it a question that we should try seriously to answer or at least understand.

The great difficulty of understanding, and communication, lies in the fact that we who are asked this question and those who ask it do not really inhabit the same universe.

You do not need to tell me that this remark smacks of artistic snobbism which is about as unattractive as any other form that snobbism can take. (If artists are snobs, it is much in the same humble way that lunatics are: not because they wish to be different, and hope and believe that they are, but because they are forever painfully struck in the face with the inescapable fact of their difference which makes them hurt and lonely enough to want to undertake the vocation of artists.)

It appears to me, sometimes, that there are only two kinds of people who live outside what E. E. Cummings has defined as "this so-called world of ours"—the artists and the insane. Of course there are those who are not practicing artists and those who have not been committed to asylums, but who have enough of one or both magical elements, lunacy and vision, to permit them also to slip sufficiently apart from "this so-called world of ours" to undertake or accept an exterior view of it. But I feel that Mr. Cummings established a highly defensible point when he stated, at least by implication, that "the everyday humdrum world, which includes me and you and millions upon millions of men and women" is pretty largely something done with mirrors, and the mirrors are the millions of eyes that look at each other and things no more penetratingly than the physical senses allow. If they are conscious of there being anything to explore beyond this *soi-disant* universe, they comfortably suppose it to be represented by the mellow tones of the pipe organ on Sundays.

In expositions of this sort it is sometimes very convenient

[43]

to invent an opposite party to an argument, as Mr. Cummings did in making the remarks I have quoted. Such an invented adversary might say to me at this point:

"I have read some of these books, like this one here, and I think they're sickening and crazy. I don't know why anybody should want to write about such diseased and perverted and fantastic creatures and try to pass them off as representative members of the human race! That's how I feel about it. But I do have this sense you talk about, as much as you do or anybody else, this sense of fearfulness or dreadfulness or whatever you want to call it. I read the newspapers and I think it's all pretty awful. I think the atom bomb is awful and I think that the confusion of the world is awful. I think that cancer is fearful, and I certainly don't look forward to the idea of dying, which I think is dreadful. I could go on forever, or at least indefinitely, giving you a list of things that I think are dreadful. And isn't that having what you call the Sense of Dreadfulness or something?"

My hesitant answer would be—"Yes, and no. Mostly no."

And then I would explain a little further, with my usual awkwardness at exposition:

"All of these things that you list as dreadful are parts of the visible, sensible phenomena of every man's experience or knowledge, but the true sense of dread is not a reaction to anything sensible or visible or even, strictly, materially, *knowable*. But rather it's a kind of spiritual intuition of something almost too incredible and shocking to talk about, which underlies the whole so-called thing. It is the uncommunicable something that we shall have to call *mystery* which is so inspiring of dread among these modern artists that we have been talking about. . . ."

Then I pause, looking into the eyes of my interlocutor, which I hope are beginning to betray some desire to believe me, and I say to him, "Am I making any better sense?"

"Maybe. But I can see it's an effort!"

"My friend, you have me where the hair is short."

"But you know, you still haven't explained why these writers have to write about crazy people doing terrible things!"

"You mean the externals they use?"

" 'Externals?' "

"You are objecting to their choice of symbols."

"Symbols, are they?"

"Of course. Art is made out of symbols the way your body is made out of vital tissue."

"Then why have they got to use—?"

"Symbols of the grotesque and the violent? Because a book is short and a man's life is long."

"That I don't understand."

"Think it over."

"You mean it's got to be more concentrated?"

"Exactly. The awfulness has to be compressed."

"But can't a writer ever get the same effect without using such God damn awful subjects?"

"I believe one writer did. The greatest of modern times, James Joyce. He managed to get the whole sense of awfulness without resorting to externals that departed on the surface from the ordinary and the familiar. But he wrote very long books, when he accomplished this incredibly difficult thing, and also he used a device that is known as the interior monologue which only he and one other great modern writer could employ without being excessively tiresome."

"What other?"

"Marcel Proust. But Proust did not ever quite dare to deliver the message of Absolute Dread. He was too much of a physical coward. The atmosphere of his work is rather womb-like. The flight into protection is very apparent."

"I guess we've talked long enough. Don't you have to get back to your subject now?"

"I have just about finished with my subject, thanks to you."

"Aren't you going to make a sort of statement that adds it up?"

"Neatly? Yes. Maybe I'd better try: here it is: *Reflections in a Golden Eye* is one of the purest and most powerful of those works which are conceived in that Sense of The Awful which is the desperate black root of nearly all significant modern art, from the *Guernica* of Picasso to the cartoons of Charles Addams. Is that all right?"

"I have quit arguing with you. So long."

It is true that this book lacks somewhat the thematic magnitude of the *Chasseur Solitaire,* but there is an equally important respect in which it is superior.

The first novel had a tendency to overflow in places as if the virtuosity of the young writer had not yet fallen under her entire control. But in the second there is an absolute mastery of design. There is a lapidary precision about the structure of this second book. Furthermore I think it succeeds more perfectly in establishing its own reality, in creating a world of its own, and this is something that primarily distinguishes the work of a great artist from that of a professional writer. In this book there is perhaps no single passage that assaults the heart so mercilessly as that scene in the earlier novel where the deaf-mute Singer stands at night outside the squalid flat that he had formerly occupied with the crazed and now dying Antonapoulos. The acute tragic sensibility of scenes like that occurred more frequently in *The Heart Is a Lonely Hunter*. Here the artistic climate is more austere. The tragedy is more distilled: a Grecian purity cools it, the eventually overwhelming impact is to a more reflective order. The key to this deliberate difference is implicit in the very title of the book. Discerning critics should have found it the opposite of a disappointment since it exhibited the one attribute which had yet to be shown in Carson McCullers's stunning array of gifts: the gift of mastery over a youthful lyricism.

I will add, however, that this second novel is still not her greatest; it is surpassed by *The Member of the Wedding,* her third novel, which combined the heartbreaking tenderness of the first with the sculptural quality of the second. But this book is in turn surpassed by a somewhat shorter work. I am speaking of *The Ballad of the Sad Cafe,* which is assuredly among the masterpieces of our language in the form of the novella.

During the two years that I have spent mostly abroad I have been impressed by the disparity that exists between Carson McCullers's reputation at home and in Europe. Translation serves as a winnowing process. The lesser and more derivative talents that have boisterously flooded our literary scene, with reputations inflated by professional politics and by shrewd commercial promotion, have somewhat obscured at home the position of more authentic talents. But in Europe the name of Carson McCullers is where it belongs, among the four or five preeminent figures in contemporary American writing.

Carson McCullers does not work rapidly. She is not coerced by the ridiculous popular idea that a good novelist turns out a book once a year. As long as five years elapsed between her second full-length novel and her third. I understand now that she has begun to work upon another. There could be no better literary news for any of us who have found, as I have found in her work, such intensity and nobility of spirit as we have not had in our prose writing since Herman Melville. In the meantime she should be reassured by the constantly more abundant evidence that the work she has already accomplished, such as this work, is not eclipsed by time, but further illumined.

The Timeless World of a Play

CARSON MCCULLERS CONCLUDES one of her lyric poems with the line: "Time, the endless idiot, runs screaming 'round the world." It is this continual rush of time, so violent that it appears to be screaming, that deprives our actual lives of so much dignity and meaning, and it is, perhaps more than anything else, the *arrest of time* which has taken place in a completed work of art that gives to certain plays their feeling of depth and significance. In the London notices of *Death of a Salesman* a certain notoriously skeptical critic made the remark that Willy Loman was the sort of man that almost any member of the audience would have kicked out of an office had he applied for a job or detained one for conversation about his troubles. The remark itself possibly holds some truth. But the implication that Willy Loman is consequently

This essay appeared in the *New York Times,* January 14, 1951, and was then used as an introduction to the first published version of *The Rose Tattoo,* New Directions, 1951.

a character with whom we have no reason to concern ourselves in drama, reveals a strikingly false conception of what plays are. Contemplation is something that exists outside of time, and so is the tragic sense. Even in the actual world of commerce, there exists in some persons a sensibility to the unfortunate situations of others, a capacity for concern and compassion, surviving from a more tender period of life outside the present whirling wire-cage of business activity. Facing Willy Loman across an office desk, meeting his nervous glance and hearing his querulous voice, we would be very likely to glance at our wrist watch and our schedule of other appointments. We would not kick him out of the office, no, but we would certainly *ease* him out with more expedition than Willy had feebly hoped for. But suppose there had been no wrist watch or office clock and suppose there had *not* been the schedule of pressing appointments, and suppose that we were not actually facing Willy across a desk—and facing a person is *not* the best way to *see* him!—suppose, in other words, that the meeting with Willy Loman had somehow occurred in a world *outside* of time. Then I think we would receive him with concern and kindness and even with respect. If the world of a play did not offer us this occasion to view its characters under that special condition of a *world without time,* then, indeed, the characters and occurrences of drama would become equally pointless, equally trivial, as corresponding meetings and happenings in life.

The classic tragedies of Greece had tremendous nobility. The actors wore great masks, movements were formal, dance-like, and the speeches had an epic quality which doubtless was as removed from the normal conversation of their contemporary society as they seem today. Yet they did not seem false to the Greek audiences: the magnitude of the events and the passions aroused by them did not seem ridiculously out of proportion to common experience. And I wonder if this was not because the Greek audiences knew, instinctively or by training, that the created world of a play is removed from that element which makes people *little* and their emotions fairly inconsequential.

Great sculpture often follows the lines of the human body: yet the repose of great sculpture suddenly transmutes those human lines to something that has an absoluteness, a purity, a beauty, which would not be possible in a living mobile form.

A play may be violent, full of motion: yet it has that special kind of repose which allows contemplation and produces the climate in which tragic importance is a possible thing, provided that certain modern conditions are met.

In actual existence the moments of love are succeeded by the moments of satiety and sleep. The sincere remark is followed by a cynical distrust. Truth is fragmentary, at best: we love and betray each other in not quite the same breath but in two breaths that occur in fairly close sequence. But the fact that passion occurred in *passing,* that it then declined into a more familiar sense of indifference, should not be regarded as proof of its inconsequence. And this is the very truth that drama wished to bring us. . . .

Whether or not we admit it to ourselves, we are all haunted by a truly awful sense of impermanence. I have always had a particularly keen sense of this at New York cocktail parties, and perhaps that is why I drink the martinis almost as fast as I can snatch them from the tray. This sense is the febrile thing that hangs in the air. Horror of insincerity, of *not meaning,* overhangs these affairs like the cloud of cigarette smoke and the hectic chatter. This horror is the only thing, almost, that is left unsaid at such functions. All social functions involving a group of people not intimately known to each other are always under this shadow. They are almost always (in an unconscious way) like that last dinner of the condemned: where steak or turkey, whatever the doomed man wants, is served in his cell as a mockingly cruel reminder of what the great-big-little-transitory world had to offer.

In a play, time is arrested in the sense of being confined. By a sort of legerdemain, events are made to remain *events,* rather than being reduced so quickly to mere *occurrences.* The audience can sit back in a comforting dusk to watch a world which is flooded with light and in which emotion and action have a dimension and dignity that they would likewise have in real existence, if only the shattering intrusion of time could be locked out.

About their lives, people ought to remember that when they are finished, everything in them will be contained in a marvelous state of repose which is the same as that which they unconsciously admired in drama. The rush is temporary. The great and only possible dignity of man lies in his power deliberately to choose certain moral values by which to live as steadfastly as if he, too, like a character in a play, were immured against the corrupting rush of time. Snatching the eternal out of the desperately fleeting is the great magic trick of human existence. As far as we know, as far as there exists any kind of empiric evidence, there is no way to beat the game of *being* against *non-being*, in which non-being is the predestined victor on realistic levels.

Yet plays in the tragic tradition offer us a view of certain moral values in violent juxtaposition. Because we do not participate, except as spectators, we can view them clearly, within the limits of our emotional equipment. These people on the stage do not return our looks. We do not have to answer their questions nor make any sign of being in company with them, nor do we have to compete with their virtues nor resist their offenses. All at once, for this reason, we are able to *see* them! Our hearts are wrung by recognition and pity, so that the dusky shell of the auditorium where we are gathered anonymously together is flooded with an almost liquid warmth of unchecked human sympathies, relieved of self-consciousness, allowed to function. . . .

Men pity and love each other more deeply than they permit themselves to know. The moment after the phone has been hung up, the hand reaches for a scratch pad and scrawls a notation: "Funeral Tuesday at five, Church of the Holy Redeemer, don't forget flowers." And the same hand is only a little shakier than usual as it reaches, some minutes later, for a highball glass that will pour a stupefaction over the kindled nerves. Fear and evasion are the two little beasts that chase each other's tails in the revolving wire-cage of our nervous world. They distract us from feeling too much about things. Time rushes toward us with its hospital tray of infinitely varied narcotics, even while it is preparing us for its inevitably fatal operation. . . .

So successfully have we disguised from ourselves the intensity of our own feelings, the sensibility of our own hearts, that plays in the tragic tradition have begun to seem untrue. For a couple of hours we may surrender ourselves to a world of fiercely illuminated values in conflict, but when the stage is covered and the auditorium lighted, almost immediately there is a recoil of disbelief. "Well, well!" we say as we shuffle back up the aisle, while the play dwindles behind us with the sudden perspective of an early Chirico painting. By the time we have arrived at Sardi's, if not as soon as we pass beneath the marquee, we have convinced ourselves once more that life has as little resemblance to the curiously stirring and meaningful occurrences on the stage as a jingle has to an elegy of Rilke.

This modern condition of his theater audience is something that an author must know in advance. The diminishing influence of life's destroyer, time, must be somehow worked into the context of his play. Perhaps it is a certain foolery, a certain distortion toward the grotesque, which will solve the problem for him. Perhaps it is only restraint, putting a mute on the strings that would like to break all bounds. But almost surely, unless he contrives in some way to relate the dimensions of his tragedy to the dimensions of a world in which time is *included*—he will be left among his magnificent debris on a dark stage, muttering to himself: "Those fools. . . ."

And if they could hear him above the clatter of tongues, glasses, chinaware, and silver, they would give him this answer: "But you have shown us a world not ravaged by time. We admire your innocence. But we have seen our photographs, past and present. Yesterday evening we passed our first wife on the street. We smiled as we spoke but we didn't really see her! It's too bad, but we know what is true and not true, and at 3 A.M. your disgrace will be in print!"

The Meaning of
The Rose Tattoo

The Rose Tattoo is the Dionysian element in human life, its mystery, its beauty, its significance. It is that glittering quicksilver that still somehow manages to slip from under the down-pressed thumbs of the enormous man in the brass-buttoned uniform and his female partner with the *pince-nez* and the chalky smelling black skirts that make you sneeze as she brushes disdainfully past you. It is the dissatisfaction with empiric evidence that makes the poet and mystic, for it is the lyric as well as the Bacchantic impulse, and although the goat is one of its most immemorial symbols, it must not be confused with mere sexuality. The element is higher and more distilled than that. Its purest form is probably manifested by children and birds in their rhapsodic moments of flight and play, especially during the last few minutes of pale blue summer dusk before they light on branches and before their mothers call from the doors, *Come home!* It is not the obedient coming home and going to bed but it is the limitless world of

This essay appeared in *Vogue*, March 15, 1951.

the dream. It is the *rosa mystica*, the light on the bare golden flesh of a god whose back is turned to us or whose face is covered and who flies away from us when we call *Wait!* and rushes past us when we try to stop him. It is the fruit of the vine that takes earth, sun, and air and distills them into juices that deprive men not of reason but of a different thing called prudence. . . .

Finally and incidentally, it is the desire of an artist to work in new forms, however awkwardly at first, to break down barriers of what he has done before and what others have done better before and after and to crash, perhaps fatally, into some area that the bell-harness and rope would like to forbid him.

It may seem curious that I have chosen a woman to be the main protagonist of a play on such a theme. But in the blind and frenzied efforts of the widow, Serafina, to comprehend the mysteries of her dead husband, we sense and learn more about him than would have been possible through direct observation of the living man, the Dionysus himself. Dionysus, being mystery, is never seen clearly. He can not be confined to memory nor an urn, nor the conventions and proprieties of a plump little seamstress who wanted to fortify her happiness with the respect of the community. It was a mistake to fill the house with dummies. It took a long while to learn that eventually the faceless dummies must be knocked over, however elaborate their trappings. It took an almost literal unclothing, a public appearance in a wine-stained rayon slip, a fierce attack on a priest and the neighbor women, to learn that the blood of the wild young daughter was better, as a memorial, than ashes kept in a crematory urn.

In its treatment of this theme the play is no doubt mo.
allusive than direct. Still more undoubtedly its theme over-
shadows the play. It is the homely light of a kitchen candle
burned in praise of a god. I prefer a play to be not a noose but
a net with fairly wide meshes. So many of its instants of
revelation are wayward flashes, not part of the plan of an
author but struck accidentally off, and perhaps these are
closest to being a true celebration of the inebriate god.

Facts about Me

I WAS BORN in the Episcopal rectory of Columbus, Miss., an old town on the Tombigbee River which was so dignified and reserved that there was a saying, only slightly exaggerated, that you had to live there a whole year before a neighbor would smile at you on the street. As my grandfather, with whom we lived, was the Episcopal clergyman, we were accepted without probation. My father, a man with the formidable name of Cornelius Coffin Williams, was a man of ancestry that came on one side, the Williams, from pioneer Tennessee stock and on the other from early settlers of Nantucket Island in New England. My mother was descended from Quakers. Roughly there was a combination of Puritan and Cavalier strains in my blood which may be accountable for the conflicting impulses I often represent in the people I write about.

This essay appeared on the jacket of the record album "Tennessee Williams Reading From His Works," Caedmon Records, 1952.

[58]

I was christened Thomas Lanier Williams. It is a nice enough name, perhaps a little too nice. It sounds like it might belong to the son of a writer who turns out sonnet sequences to Spring. As a matter of fact, my first literary award was $25.00 from a Woman's Club for doing exactly that, three sonnets dedicated to Spring. I hasten to add that I was still pretty young. Under that name I published a good deal of lyric poetry which was a bad imitation of Edna Millay. When I grew up I realized this poetry wasn't much good and I felt the name had been compromised so I changed it to Tennessee Williams, the justification being mainly that the Williamses had fought the Indians for Tennessee and I had already discovered that the life of a young writer was going to be something similar to the defense of a stockade against a band of savages.

When I was about twelve, my father, a travelling salesman, was appointed to an office position in St. Louis and so we left the rectory and moved north. It was a tragic move. Neither my sister nor I could adjust ourselves to life in a Midwestern city. The schoolchildren made fun of our Southern speech and manners. I remember gangs of kids following me home yelling "Sissy!" and home was not a very pleasant refuge. It was a perpetually dim little apartment in a wilderness of identical brick and concrete structures with no grass and no trees nearer than the park. In the South we had never been conscious of the fact that we were economically less fortunate than others. We lived as well as anyone else. But in St. Louis we suddenly discovered there were two kinds of people, the rich and the poor, and that we belonged more to the latter. If we walked far enough west we came into a region of fine residences set in beautiful lawns. But where we lived, to which we must always return, were ugly rows of apartment buildings the color of dried blood and mustard. If I had been born to this situation I might not have resented it deeply. But it was forced upon my consciousness at the most sensitive age of childhood. It produced a shock and a rebellion that has grown into an inherent part of my work. It was the beginning of the social consciousness which I think has marked most of my writing. I am glad that I received this bitter education for I don't think any writer has much purpose back of him unless he feels bitterly the inequities of the society he lives in. I have no acquaintance with political and social dialectics. If you ask what my politics are, I am a Humanitarian.

That is the social background of my life!

I entered college during the great American depression and after a couple of years I couldn't afford to continue but had to drop out and take a clerical job in the shoe company that employed my father. The two years I spent in that corporation were indescribable torment to me as an individual but of immense value to me as a writer for they gave me first-hand knowledge of what it means to be a small wage earner in a hopelessly routine job. I had been writing since childhood and I continued writing while I was employed by the shoe company. When I came home from work I would tank up on black coffee so I could remain awake most of the night, writing short stories which I could not sell. Gradually my health broke down. One day, coming home from work, I collapsed and was removed to the hospital. The doctor said

[60]

I couldn't go back to the shoe company. Soon as that was settled I recovered and went back South to live with my grandparents in Memphis where they had moved since my grandfather's retirement from the ministry. Then I began to have a little success with my writing. I became self-sufficient. I put myself through two more years of college and got a B.A. degree at the University of Iowa in 1938. Before then and for a couple of years afterwards I did a good deal of travelling around and I held a great number of part-time jobs of great diversity. It is hard to put the story in correct chronology for the last ten years of my life are a dizzy kaleidoscope. I don't quite believe all that has happened to me, it seems it must have happened to five or ten other people.

My first real recognition came in 1940 when I received a Rockefeller fellowship and wrote *Battle of Angels* which was produced by the Theatre Guild at the end of that year with Miriam Hopkins in the leading role. It closed in Boston during the tryout run but I have rewritten it a couple of times since then and still have faith in it. My health was so impaired that I landed in 4F after a medical examination of about five minutes' duration. My jobs in this period included running an all-night elevator in a big apartment-hotel, waiting on tables and reciting verse in the Village, working as a tele-type operator for the U.S. Engineers in Jacksonville, Florida, waiter and cashier for a small restaurant in New Orleans, ushering at the Strand Theatre on Broadway. All the while I kept on writing, writing, not with any hope of making a living at it but because I found no other means of expressing things that seemed to demand expression. There was never a

[61]

moment when I did not find life to be immeasurably exciting to experience and to witness, however difficult it was to sustain.

From a $17.00 a week job as a movie usher I was suddenly shipped off to Hollywood where MGM paid me $250.00 a week. I saved enough money out of my six months there to keep me while I wrote *The Glass Menagerie*. I don't think the story from that point on, requires any detailed consideration.

Foreword to

Camino Real

It is amazing and frightening how completely one's whole being becomes absorbed in the making of a play. It is almost as if you were frantically constructing another world while the world that you live in dissolves beneath your feet, and that your survival depends on completing this construction at least one second before the old habitation collapses.

More than any other work that I have done, this play has seemed to me like the construction of another world, a separate existence. Of course, it is nothing more nor less than my conception of the time and world that I live in, and its people are mostly archetypes of certain basic attitudes and qualities with those mutations that would occur if they had continued along the road to this hypothetical terminal point in it.

This essay was written prior to the Broadway premiere of *Camino Real* and published in the *New York Times*, Sunday, March 15, 1953. It is also included in the published version of the play, New Directions, 1953.

A convention of the play is existence outside of time in a place of no specific locality. If you regard it that way, I suppose it becomes an elaborate allegory, but in New Haven we opened directly across the street from a movie theater that was showing *Peter Pan* in Technicolor and it did not seem altogether inappropriate to me. Fairy tales nearly always have some simple moral lesson of good and evil, but that is not the secret of their fascination any more, I hope, than the philosophical import that might be distilled from the fantasies of *Camino Real* is the principal element of its appeal.

To me the appeal of this work is its unusual degree of freedom. When it began to get under way I felt a new sensation of release, as if I could "ride out" like a tenor sax taking the breaks in a Dixieland combo or a piano in a bop session. You may call it self-indulgence, but I was not doing it merely for myself. I could not have felt a purely private thrill of release unless I had hope of sharing this experience with lots and lots of audiences to come.

My desire was to give these audiences my own sense of something wild and unrestricted that ran like water in the mountains, or clouds changing shape in a gale, or the continually dissolving and transforming images of a dream. This sort of freedom is not chaos nor anarchy. On the contrary, it is the result of painstaking design, and in this work I have given more conscious attention to form and construction than I have in any work before. Freedom is not achieved simply by working freely.

Elia Kazan was attracted to this work mainly, I believe, for the same reason—its freedom and mobility of form. I know that we have kept saying the word "flight" to each other as if the play were merely an abstraction of the impulse to fly, and most of the work out of town, his in staging, mine in cutting and revising, has been with this impulse in mind: the achievement of a continual flow. Speech after speech and bit after bit that were nice in themselves have been remorselessly blasted out of the script and its staging wherever they seemed to obstruct or divert this flow.

There have been plenty of indications already that this play will exasperate and confuse a certain number of people which we hope is not so large as the number it is likely to please. At each performance a number of people have stamped out of the auditorium, with little regard for those whom they have had to crawl over, almost as if the building had caught on fire, and there have been sibilant noises on the way out and demands for money back if the cashier was foolish enough to remain in his box.

I am at a loss to explain this phenomenon, and if I am being facetious about one thing, I am being quite serious about another when I say that I had never for one minute supposed that the play would seem obscure and confusing to anyone who was willing to meet it even less than halfway. It was a costly production, and for this reason I had to read it aloud, together with a few of the actors on one occasion, before large groups of prospective backers, before the funds to produce it were in the till. It was only then that I came up against the disconcerting surprise that some people would think that the play needed clarification.

My attitude is intransigent. I still don't agree that it needs any explanation. Some poet has said that a poem should not mean but be. Of course, a play is not a poem, not even a poetic play has quite the same license as a poem. But to go to *Camino Real* with the inflexible demands of a logician is unfair to both parties.

In Philadelphia a young man from a literary periodical saw the play and then cross-examined me about all its dream-like images. He had made a list of them while he watched the play, and afterward at my hotel he brought out the list and asked me to explain the meaning of each one. I can't deny that I use a lot of those things called symbols but being a self-defensive creature, I say that symbols are nothing but the natural speech of drama.

We all have in our conscious and unconscious minds a great vocabulary of images, and I think all human communication is based on these images as are our dreams; and a symbol in a play has only one legitimate purpose, which is to say a thing more directly and simply and beautifully than it could be said in words.

I hate writing that is a parade of images for the sake of images; I hate it so much that I close a book in disgust when it keeps on saying one thing is like another; I even get disgusted with poems that make nothing but comparisons between one thing and another. But I repeat that symbols, when used respectfully, are the purest language of plays. Sometimes it would take page after tedious page of exposition to put across an idea that can be said with an object or a gesture on the lighted stage.

To take one case in point: the battered portmanteau of Jacques Casanova is hurled from the balcony of a luxury hotel when his remittance check fails to come through. While the portmanteau is still in the air, he shouts: "Careful, I have—"

—and when it has crashed to the street he continues—"fragile—mementoes. . . ." I suppose that is a symbol, at least it is an object used to express as directly and vividly as possible certain things which could be said in pages of dull talk.

As for those patrons who departed before the final scene, I offer myself this tentative bit of solace: that these theater-goers may be a little domesticated in their theatrical tastes. A cage represents security as well as confinement to a bird that has grown used to being in it; and when a theatrical work kicks over the traces with such apparent insouciance, security seems challenged and, instead of participating in its sense of freedom, one out of a certain number of playgoers will rush back out to the more accustomed implausibility of the street he lives on.

To modify this effect of complaisance I would like to admit to you quite frankly that I can't say with any personal conviction that I have written a good play; I only know that I have felt a release in this work which I wanted you to feel with me.

Afterword to
Camino Real

ONCE IN A WHILE someone will say to me that he would rather wait for a play to come out as a book than see a live performance of it, where he would be distracted from its true values, if it has any, by so much that is mere spectacle and sensation and consequently must be meretricious and vulgar. There are plays meant for reading. I have read them. I have read the works of "thinking playwrights" as distinguished from us who are permitted only to feel, and probably read them earlier and appreciated them as much as those who invoke their names nowadays like the incantation of Aristophanes's frogs. But the incontinent blaze of a live theater, a theater meant for seeing and for feeling, has never been and never will be extinguished by a bucket brigade of critics, new or old, bearing vessels that range from cut glass punch bowl to Haviland teacup. And in my dissident opinion, a play in a book is only the shadow of a play and not even a clear

The Afterword, dated June 1, 1953, was included in the first published version of *Camino Real,* New Directions, 1953.

shadow of it. Those who did not like *Camino Real* on the stage will not be likely to form a higher opinion of it in print, for of all the works I have written, this one was meant most for the vulgarity of performance. The printed script of a play is hardly more than an architect's blueprint of a house not yet built or built and destroyed.

The color, the grace and levitation, the structural pattern in motion, the quick interplay of live beings, suspended like fitful lightning in a cloud, these things are the play, not words on paper, nor thoughts and ideas of an author, those shabby things snatched off basement counters at Gimbel's.

My own creed as a playwright is fairly close to that expressed by the painter in Shaw's play *The Doctor's Dilemma:* "I believe in Michelangelo, Velásquez and Rembrandt; in the might of design, the mystery of color, the redemption of all things by beauty everlasting and the message of art that has made these hands blessed. Amen."

How much art his hands were blessed with or how much mine are, I don't know, but that art is a blessing is certain and that it contains its message is also certain, and I feel, as the painter did, that the message lies in those abstract beauties of form and color and line, to which I would add light and motion.

In these following pages are only the formula by which a play could exist.

Dynamic is a word in disrepute at the moment, and so, I suppose, is the word *organic,* but those terms still define the dramatic values that I value most and which I value more as they are more deprecated by the ones self-appointed to save what they have never known.

[69]

Critic Says "Evasion,"
Writer Says "Mystery"

IN HIS REVIEWS of *Cat on a Hot Tin Roof*, Mr. Walter Kerr has spoken of an "evasiveness" on my part in dealing with certain questions in the play, mainly questions of character, pertinent mostly to the character of the young male protagonist, Brick Pollitt. This is not the first time that I've been suspected of dodging issues in my treatment of play characters. Critics complained, sometimes, of ambiguities in *Streetcar*. Certainly there were many divergent ideas of Blanche's character and many widely differing interpretations in the playing of her character among the many productions I saw at home and abroad. She was often referred to as a prostitute, often as a dipso or a nympho or liar.

The truth about human character in a play, as in life, varies with the variance of experience and viewpoint of those that view it. No two members of an audience ever leave a theater, after viewing a play that deals with any degree of

This essay appeared in the *New York Herald Tribune*, April 17, 1955.

complexity in character, with identical interpretations of the characters dealt with. This is as it should be. I know full well the defenses and rationalizations of beleaguered writers, a defensive species, but I still feel that I deal unsparingly with what I feel is the truth of character. I would never evade it for the sake of evasion, because I was in any way reluctant to reveal what I know of the truth.

But ambiguity is sometimes deliberate, and for artistically defensible reasons, I can best answer Mr. Kerr's objection by a quote from the manuscript of the play which is not yet available to readers, but will be in a few weeks. It is a long note that occurs in the second act, at the point where Big Daddy alludes to the charge of abnormality in Brick's relation to his dead friend, Skipper:

Brick's resolute detachment is at last broken through. His heart is accelerated; his forehead sweat-beaded; his breath becomes more rapid and his voice hoarse. The thing they're discussing, timidly and painfully on the side of Big Daddy, fiercely, violently on Brick's side, is the inadmissible thing that Skipper and Brick would rather die than live with. The fact that if it existed it had to be disavowed to "keep face" in the world they lived in, a world of popular heroes, may be at the heart of the "mendacity" that Brick drinks to kill his disgust with. It may be the root of his collapse. Or it may be only a single manifestation of it, not even the most important. The bird that I hope to catch in the net of this play is not the solution of one man's psychological problem. I'm trying to catch the true quality of experience in a group of people, that cloudy, flickering, evanescent—fiercely charged! —interplay of live human beings in the thundercloud of a common crisis. Some mystery should be left in the revelation of character in a play, just as a great deal of mystery is always left in the revelation of character in life, even in one's own character to himself. This does not absolve the playwright of his duty to observe and probe as clearly and deeply as he *legitimately* can: but it should steer him away from "pat" conclusions, facile definitions, which make a play just a play, not a snare for the truth of human experience.

This, I believe, states clearly my defense of these so-called ambiguities of character in my plays. The point is, of course, arguable. You may prefer to be told precisely what to believe about every character in a play; you may prefer to know precisely what will be the future course of their lives, happy or disastrous or anywhere in between.

Then I am not your playwright. My characters make my play. I always start with them, they take spirit and body in my mind. Nothing that they say or do is arbitrary or invented. They build the play about them like spiders weaving their webs, sea creatures making their shells. I live with them for a year and a half or two years and I know them far better than I know myself, since I created them and not myself.

But still they must have that quality of life which is shadowy. Was Blanche Dubois a liar? She told many lies in the course of *Streetcar* and yet at heart she was truthful. Was Brick homosexual? He probably—no, I would even say quite certainly—went no further in physical expression than clasping Skipper's hand across the space between their twin beds in hotel rooms—and yet his sexual nature was not innately "normal."

Did Brick love Maggie? He says with unmistakable conviction: "One man has one great good true thing in his life, one great good thing which is true. I had friendship with Skipper, not love with you, Maggie, but friendship with Skipper. . . ."—but can we doubt that he was warmed and charmed by this delightful girl, with her vivacity, her humor, her very admirable courage and pluckiness and tenacity, which are almost the essence of life itself?

Of course, now that he has really resigned from life, retired from competition, her anxious voice, strident with the heat of combat, is unpleasantly, sometimes even odiously, disturbing to him. But Brick's overt sexual adjustment was, and must always remain, a heterosexual one. He will go back to Maggie for sheer animal comfort, even if she did not make him dependent on her for such creature comforts as only a devoted slave can provide. He is her dependent. As Strindberg said: "They call it love-hatred, and it hails from the pit. . . ."

Frankly, I don't want people to leave the Morosco Theatre knowing everything about all the characters they have witnessed that night in violent interplay, I don't want them to be quite certain what will happen to these characters that night or in the morning. Because they themselves, when they step out of the Morosco, cannot be certain that a truck will not run them down while they are hailing a taxi. I give them views, but not certainties.

Every moment of human existence is alive with uncertainty. You may call it ambiguity, you may even call it evasion. I want them to leave the Morosco as they do leave it each night, feeling that they have met with a vividly allusive,

as well as disturbingly elusive, fragment of human experience, one that not only points at truth but at the mysteries of
it, much as they will leave this world when they leave it, still
wondering somewhat about what happened to them, and for
what reason or purpose.

Person — to — Person

Of course it is a pity that so much of all creative work is so closely related to the personality of the one who does it.

It is sad and embarrassing and unattractive that those emotions that stir him deeply enough to demand expression, and to charge their expression with some measure of light and power, are nearly all rooted, however changed in their surface, in the particular and sometimes peculiar concerns of the artist himself, that special world, the passions and images of it that each of us weaves about him from birth to death, a web of monstrous complexity, spun forth at a speed that is incalculable to a length beyond measure, from the spider mouth of his own singular perceptions.

It is a lonely idea, a lonely condition, so terrifying to

This essay appeared in the *New York Times* Sunday Drama Section, 1955. It was subsequently used as an introduction to the first published edition of *Cat on a Hot Tin Roof,* New Directions, 1955.

[75]

think of that we usually don't. And so we talk to each other, write and wire each other, call each other short and long distance across land and sea, clasp hands with each other at meeting and at parting, fight each other and even destroy each other because of this always somewhat thwarted effort to break through walls to each other. As a character in a play once said, "We're all of us sentenced to solitary confinement inside our own skins."

Personal lyricism is the outcry of prisoner to prisoner from the cell in solitary where each is confined for the duration of his life.

I once saw a group of little girls on a Mississippi sidewalk, all dolled up in their mothers' and sisters' cast-off finery, old raggedy ball gowns and plumed hats and high-heeled slippers, enacting a meeting of ladies in a parlor with a perfect mimicry of polite Southern gush and simper. But one child was not satisfied with the attention paid her enraptured performance by the others, they were too involved in their own performances to suit her, so she stretched out her skinny arms and threw back her skinny neck and shrieked to the deaf heavens and her equally oblivious playmates, "Look at me, look at me, look at me!"

And then her mother's high-heeled slippers threw her off balance and she fell to the sidewalk in a great howling tangle of soiled white satin and torn pink net, and still nobody looked at her.

I wonder if she is not, now, a Southern writer.

Of course it is not only Southern writers, of lyrical bent, who engage in such histrionics and shout, "Look at me!" Perhaps it is a parable of all artists. And not always do we topple over and land in a tangle of trappings that don't fit us. However, it is well to be aware of that peril, and not to content yourself with a demand for attention, to know that out of your personal lyricism, your sidewalk histrionics, something has to be created that will not only attract observers but participants in the performance.

I try very hard to do that.

The fact that I want you to observe what I do for your possible pleasure and to give you knowledge of things that I feel I may know better than you, because my world is different from yours, as different as every man's world is from the world of others, is not enough excuse for a personal lyricism that has not yet mastered its necessary trick of rising above the singular to the plural concern, from personal to general import. But for years and years now, which may have passed like a dream because of this obsession, I have been trying to learn how to perform this trick and make it truthful, and sometimes I feel that I am able to do it. Sometimes, when the enraptured street-corner performer in me cries out "Look at me!" I feel that my hazardous footwear and fantastic regalia may not quite throw me off balance. Then, suddenly, you fellow performers in the sidewalk show may turn to give me your attention and allow me to hold it, at least for the interval between 8:40 and 11 something P.M.

Eleven years ago this month of March, when I was far closer than I knew, only nine months away from that long-delayed, but always expected, something that I lived for, the time when I would first catch and hold an audience's attention, I wrote my first preface to a long play. The final paragraph went like this:

> There is too much to say and not enough time to say it. Nor is there power enough. I am not a good writer. Sometimes I am a very bad writer indeed. There is hardly a successful writer in the field who cannot write circles around me . . . but I think of writing as something more organic than words, something closer to being and action. I want to work more and more with a more plastic theater than the one I have (worked with) before. I have never for one moment doubted that there are people—millions!—to say things to. We come to each other, gradually, but with love. It is the short reach of my arms that hinders, not the length and multiplicity of theirs. With love and with honesty, the embrace is inevitable."

This characteristically emotional, if not rhetorical, statement of mine at that time seems to suggest that I thought of myself as having a highly personal, even intimate relationship with people who go to see plays. I did and I still do. A morbid shyness once prevented me from having much direct communication with people, and possibly that is why I began to write to them plays and stories. But even now when that tongue-locking, face-flushing, silent crouching timidity has worn off with the passage of the troublesome youth that it sprang from, I still find it somehow easier to "level with" crowds of strangers in the hushed twilight of orchestra and balcony sections of theaters than with individuals across a table from me. Their being strangers somehow makes them more familiar and more approachable, easier to talk to.

Of course I know that I have sometimes presumed too much upon corresponding sympathies and interest in those to whom I talk boldly, and this has led to rejections that were painful and costly enough to inspire more prudence. But when I weigh one thing against another, an easy liking against a hard respect, the balance always tips the same way, and whatever the risk of being turned a cold shoulder, I still don't want to talk to people only about the surface aspects of their lives, the sort of things that acquaintances laugh and chatter about on ordinary social occasions.

I feel that they get plenty of that, and heaven knows so do I, before and after the little interval of time in which I have their attention and say what I have to say to them. The discretion of social conversation, even among friends, is exceeded only by the discretion of "the deep six," that grave wherein nothing is mentioned at all. Emily Dickinson, that lyrical spinster of Amherst, Massachusetts, who wore a strict and savage heart on a taffeta sleeve, commented wryly on that kind of posthumous discourse among friends in these lines:

> I died for Beauty—but was scarce
> Adjusted in the Tomb
> When One who died for Truth, was lain
> In an adjoining Room—
>
> He questioned softly "Why I failed"?
> "For Beauty", I replied—
> "And I—for truth—Themself are one—
> We brethren are", He said—
>
> And so, as Kinsmen, met a Night—
> We talked between the Rooms—

Until the Moss had reached our lips—
And covered up—our names—

Meanwhile!—I want to go on talking to you as freely and intimately about what we live and die for as if I knew you better than anyone else whom you know.

The Past, the Present, and the Perhaps

ONE ICY BRIGHT winter morning in the last week of 1940, my brave representative, Audrey Wood, and I were crossing the Common in Boston, from an undistinguished hotel on one side to the grandeur of the Ritz-Carlton on the other. We had just read in the morning notices of *Battle of Angels,* which had opened at the Wilbur the evening before. As we crossed the Common there was a series of loud reports like gunfire from the street that we were approaching, and one of us said, "My God, they're shooting at us!"

We were still laughing, a bit hysterically, as we entered the Ritz-Carlton suite in which the big brass of the Theatre Guild and director Margaret Webster were waiting for us with that special air of gentle gravity that hangs over the demise of a play so much like the atmosphere that hangs over a

This essay first appeared in the *New York Times,* March 17, 1957, and was then used as a foreword to the published version of *Orpheus Descending* (with *Battle of Angels*), New Directions, 1958.

home from which a living soul has been snatched by the Reaper.

Not present was little Miriam Hopkins, who was understandably shattered and cloistered after the events of the evening before, in which a simulated on-stage fire had erupted clouds of smoke so realistically over both stage and auditorium that a lot of Theatre Guild first-nighters had fled choking from the Wilbur before the choking star took her bows, which were about the quickest and most distracted that I have seen in a theater.

It was not that morning that I was informed that the show must close. That morning I was only told that the play must be cut to the bone. I came with a rewrite of the final scene and I remember saying, heroically, "I will crawl on my belly through brimstone if you will substitute this." The response was gently evasive. It was a few mornings later that I received the *coup de grace,* the announcement that the play would close at the completion of its run in Boston. On that occasion I made an equally dramatic statement, on a note of anguish. "You don't seem to see that I put my heart into this play!"

It was Miss Webster who answered with a remark I have never forgotten and yet never heeded. She said, "You must not wear your heart on your sleeve for daws to peck at!" Someone else said, "At least you are not out of pocket." I don't think I had any answer for that one, any more than I had anything in my pocket to be out of.

Well, in the end, when the Boston run was finished, I was given a check for $200 and told to get off somewhere and rewrite the play. I squandered half of this subsidy on the first of four operations performed on a cataracted left eye, and the other half took me to Key West for the rewrite. It was a long rewrite. In fact, it is still going on, though the two hundred bucks are long gone.

Why have I stuck so stubbornly to this play? For seventeen years, in fact? Well, nothing is more precious to anybody than the emotional record of his youth, and you will find the trail of my sleeve-worn heart in this completed play that I now call *Orpheus Descending*. On its surface it was and still is the tale of a wild-spirited boy who wanders into a conventional community of the South and creates the commotion of a fox in a chicken coop.

But beneath that now familiar surface, it is a play about unanswered questions that haunt the hearts of people and the difference between continuing to ask them, a difference represented by the four major protagonists of the play, and the acceptance of prescribed answers that are not answers at all, but expedient adaptations or surrender to a state of quandary.

Battle was actually my fifth long play, but the first to be given a professional production. Two of the others, *Candles to the Sun* and *Fugitive Kind,* were produced by a brilliant, but semiprofessional group called The Mummers of St. Louis. A third one, called *Spring Storm,* was written for the late Prof. E. C. Mabie's seminar in playwriting at the University of Iowa, and I read it aloud, appropriately in the spring.

When I had finished reading, the good professor's eyes had a glassy look as though he had drifted into a state of trance. There was a long and all but unendurable silence. Everyone seemed more or less embarrassed. At last the professor pushed back his chair, thus dismissing the seminar, and remarked casually and kindly, "Well, we all have to paint our nudes!" And this is the only reference that I can remember anyone making to the play. That is, in the playwriting class, but I do remember that the late Lemuel Ayers, who was a graduate student at Iowa that year, read it and gave me sufficient praise for its dialogue and atmosphere to reverse my decision to give up the theater in favor of my other occupation of waiting on tables, or more precisely, handing out trays in the cafeteria of the State Hospital.

Then there was Chicago for a while and a desperate effort to get on the W. P. A. Writers' Project, which didn't succeed, for my work lacked "social content" or "protest" and I couldn't prove that my family was destitute and I still had, in those days, a touch of refinement in my social behavior which made me seem frivolous and decadent to the conscientiously roughhewn pillars of the Chicago Project.

And so I drifted back to St. Louis, again, and wrote my fourth long play which was the best of the lot. It was called *Not About Nightingales* and it concerned prison life, and I have never written anything since then that could compete with it in violence and horror, for it was based on something that actually occurred along about that time, the literal roasting alive of a group of intransigent convicts sent for correction to a hot room called "The Klondike."

I submitted it to The Mummers of St. Louis and they were eager to perform it but they had come to the end of their economic tether and had to disband at this point.

Then there was New Orleans and another effort, while waiting on tables in a restaurant where meals cost only two-bits, to get on a Writers' Project or the Theatre Project, again unsuccessful.

And then there was a wild and wonderful trip to California with a young clarinet player. We ran out of gas in El Paso, also out of cash, and it seemed for days that we would never go farther, but my grandmother was an "easy touch" and I got a letter with a $10 bill stitched neatly to one of the pages, and we continued westward.

In the Los Angeles area, in the summer of 1939, I worked for a while at Clark's Bootery in Culver City, within sight of the M-G-M studio and I lived on a pigeon ranch, and I rode between the two, a distance of ten miles, on a secondhand bicycle that I bought for $5.

Then a most wonderful thing happened. While in New Orleans I had heard about a play contest being conducted by the Group Theatre of New York. I submitted all four of the long plays I have mentioned that preceded *Battle of Angels,* plus a group of one-acts called *American Blues.* One fine day I received, when I returned to the ranch on my bike, a telegram saying that I had won a special award of $100 for the one-acts, and it was signed by Harold Clurman, Molly Day Thacher, who is the present Mrs. Elia Kazan, and that fine writer, Irwin Shaw, the judges of the contest.

I retired from Clark's Bootery and from picking squabs at the pigeon ranch. And the clarinet player and I hopped on our bicycles and rode all the way down to Tiajuana and back as far as Laguna Beach, where we obtained, rent free, a small cabin on a small ranch in return for taking care of the poultry.

We lived all that summer on the $100 from the Group

Theatre and I think it was the happiest summer of my life. All the days were pure gold, the nights were starry, and I looked so young, or carefree, that they would sometimes refuse to sell me a drink because I did not appear to have reached twenty-one. But toward the end of the summer, maybe only because it was the end of the summer as well as the end of the $100, the clarinet player became very moody and disappeared without warning into the San Bernardino Mountains to commune with his soul in solitude, and there was nothing left in the cabin in the canyon but a bag of dried peas.

how Black lived Before going to see Stella

I lived on stolen eggs and avocados and dried peas for a week, and also on a faint hope stirred by a letter from a lady in New York whose name was Audrey Wood, who had taken hold of all those plays that I had submitted to the Group Theatre contest, and told me that it might be possible to get me one of the Rockefeller Fellowships, or grants, of $1,000 which were being passed out to gifted young writers at that time. And I began to write *Battle of Angels,* a lyric play about memories and the loneliness of them. Although my beloved grandmother was living on the pension of a retired minister (I believe it was only $85 a month in those days), and her meager earnings as a piano instructor, she once again stitched some bills to a page of a letter, and I took a bus to St. Louis. *Battle of Angels* was finished late that fall and sent to Miss Wood.

One day the phone rang and, in a terrified tone, my mother told me that it was long distance, for me. The voice was Audrey Wood's. Mother waited, shakily, in the doorway. When I hung up I said, quietly, "Rockefeller has given me a

$1,000 grant and they want me to come to New York." For the first time since I had known her, my mother burst into tears. "I am so happy," she said. It was all she could say.

And so you see it is a very old play that *Orpheus Descending* has come out of, but a play is never an old one until you quit working on it and I have never quit working on this one, not even now. It never went into the trunk, it always stayed on the workbench, and I am not presenting it now because I have run out of ideas or material for completely new work. I am offering it this season because I honestly believe that it is finally finished. About seventy-five percent of it is new writing, but, what is much more important, I believe that I have now finally managed to say in it what I wanted to say, and I feel that it now has in it a sort of emotional bridge between those early years described in this article and my present state of existence as a playwright.

So much for the past and present. The future is called "perhaps," which is the only possible thing to call the future. And the important thing is not to allow that to scare you.

The World I Live In

TENNESSEE WILLIAMS
INTERVIEWS HIMSELF

Question. Can we talk frankly?

Answer. There's no other way we can talk.

Q. Perhaps you know that when your first successful play, *The Glass Menagerie,* was revived early this season, a majority of the reviewers felt that it was still the best play you have written, although it is now twelve years old?

A. Yes, I read all my play notices and criticisms, even those that say that I write for money and that my primary appeal is to brutal and ugly instincts.

Q. Where there is so much smoke—!

A. A fire smokes the most when you start pouring water on it.

Q. But surely you'll admit that there's been a disturbing

This essay appeared in the *London Observer*, April 7, 1957.

note of harshness and coldness and violence and anger in your more recent works?

A. I think, without planning to do so, I have followed the developing tension and anger and violence of the world and time that I live in through my own steadily increasing tension as a writer and person.

Q. Then you admit that this "developing tension," as you call it, is a reflection of a condition in yourself?

A. Yes.

Q. A morbid condition?

A. Yes.

Q. Perhaps verging on the psychotic?

A. I guess my work has always been a kind of psycho-therapy for me.

Q. But how can you expect audiences to be impressed by plays and other writings that are created as a release for the tensions of a possible or incipient madman?

A. It releases their own.

Q. Their own what?

A. Increasing tensions, verging on the psychotic.

Q. You think the world's going mad?

A. Going? I'd say nearly gone! As the Gypsy said in *Camino Real*, the world is a funny paper read backwards. And that way it isn't so funny.

Q. How far do you think you can go with this tortured view of the world?

A. As far as the world can go in its tortured condition, maybe that far, but no further.

Q. You don't expect audiences and critics to go along with you, do you?

[89]

A. No.

Q. Then why do you push and pull them that way?

A. I go that way. I don't push or pull anyone with me.

Q. Yes, but you hope to continue to have people listen to you, don't you?

A. Naturally I hope to.

Q. Even if you throw them off by the violence and horror of your works?

A. Haven't you noticed that people are dropping all around you, like moths out of season, as the result of the present plague of violence and horror in this world and time that we live in?

Q. But you're an entertainer, with artistic pretensions, and people are not entertained any more by cats on hot tin roofs and Baby Dolls and passengers on crazy streetcars!

A. Then let them go to the musicals and the comedies. I'm not going to change my ways. It's hard enough for me to write what I want to write without me trying to write what you say they want me to write which I don't want to write.

Q. Do you have any positive message, in your opinion?

A. Indeed I do think that I do.

Q. Such as what?

A. The crying, almost screaming, need of a great world-wide human effort to know ourselves and each other a great deal better, well enough to concede that no man has a monopoly on right or virtue any more than any man has a corner on duplicity and evil and so forth. If people, and races and nations, would start with that self-manifest truth, then I think that the world could sidestep the sort of corruption which I have involuntarily chosen as the basic, allegorical theme of my plays as a whole.

Q. You sound as if you felt quite detached and superior to this process of corruption in society.

A. I have never written about any kind of vice which I can't observe in myself.

Q. But you accuse society, as a whole, of succumbing to a deliberate mendacity, and you appear to find yourself separate from it as a writer.

A. As a writer, yes, but not as a person.

Q. Do you think this is a peculiar virtue of yours as a writer?

A. I'm not sentimental about writers. But I'm inclined to think that most writers, and most other artists, too, are primarily motivated in their desperate vocation by a desire to find and to separate truth from the complex of lies and evasions they live in, and I think that this impulse is what makes their work not so much a profession as a vocation, a true "calling."

Q. Why don't you write about nice people? Haven't you ever known any nice people in your life?

A. My theory about nice people is so simple that I am embarrassed to say it.

Q. Please say it!

A. Well, I've never met one that I couldn't love if I completely knew him and understood him, and in my work I have at least tried to arrive at knowledge and understanding.

I don't believe in "original sin." I don't believe in "guilt." I don't believe in villians or heroes—only right or wrong ways that individuals have taken, not by choice but by necessity or by certain still-uncomprehended influences in themselves, their circumstances, and their antecedents.

This is so simple I'm ashamed to say it, but I'm sure it's true. In fact, I would bet my life on it! And that's why I don't understand why our propaganda machines are always trying to teach us, to persuade us, to hate and fear other people on the same little world that we live in.

Why don't we meet these people and get to know them as I try to meet and know people in my plays? This sounds terribly vain and egotistical.

I don't want to end on such a note. Then what shall I say? That I know that I am a minor artist who has happened to write one or two major works? I can't even say which they are. It doesn't matter. I have said my say. I may still say it again, or I may shut up now. It doesn't depend on you, it depends entirely on me, and the operation of chance or Providence in my life.

Author and Director:
A Delicate Situation

WHETHER HE LIKES IT or not, a writer for the stage must face the fact that the making of a play is, finally, a collaborative venture, and plays have rarely achieved a full-scale success without being in some manner raised above their manuscript level by the brilliant gifts of actors, directors, designers, and frequently even the seasoned theatrical instincts of their producers. I often wonder, for personal instance, if *The Glass Menagerie* might not have been a mere *succès d'estime*, snobbishly remembered by a small coterie, if Laurette Taylor had not poured into it her startling light and power, or if, without the genius of Kazan, *A Streetcar Named Desire* could have been kept on the tracks in those dangerous, fast curves it made here and there, or if the same genius was not requisite to making *Cat on a Hot Tin Roof* acceptable to a theater public which is so squeamish about a naked study of life.

This article appeared in *Playbill,* September 30, 1957.

A playwright's attitude toward his fellow workers goes through a cycle of three main phases. When he is just beginning in his profession, he is submissive mostly out of intimidation, for he is "nobody" and almost everybody that he works with is "somebody." He is afraid to assert himself, even when demands are made on him which, complied with, might result in a distortion of his work. He will permit lines, speeches, sometimes even whole scenes to be cut from his script because a director has found them difficult to direct or an actor has found them difficult to act. He will put in or build up a scene for a star at the sacrifice of the play's just proportions and balance. A commercial producer can sometimes even bully him into softening the denouement of his play with the nearly always wrong idea that this will improve its chances at the box office. Or if he is suddenly driven to resistance, he is unable to offer it with a cool head and a tactful tongue. Intimidation having bottled him up until now, he now pops off with unnecessary violence, he flips his lid. That's the first phase of the cycle. The second is entered when the playwright has scored his first notable success. Then the dog has his day. From intimidation he passes into the opposite condition. All of a sudden he is the great, uncompromising Purist, feeling that all ideas but his own are threats to the integrity of his work. Being suddenly a "Name" playwright, explosions of fury are no longer necessary for him to get his way. Now that he has some weight, he throws it around with the assured nonchalance of a major league pitcher warming up by the dugout. When his script is submitted to a producer by his representatives, it is not unlike the bestowal of a crown in heaven, there is a sanctified solemnity and hush about the proceedings. The tacit implication is: Here it is; take it or leave it; it will not be altered, since the slightest alteration would be nearly as sacrilegious as a revision of the Holy Scriptures.

Some playwrights are arrested at this second phase of the cycle, which is really only an aggravated reaction to the first, but sometimes the inevitable eventuality of an important failure after an important success or series of successes, will result in a moderation of the playwright's embattled ego. The temple or citadel of totally unsullied self-expression has not proven as secure a refuge as it seemed to him when he first marched triumphantly into it. It may take only one failure, it may take two or three, to persuade him that his single assessment of his work is fallible, and meanwhile, if he is not hopelessly paranoiac, he has come to learn of the existence of vitally creative minds in other departments of theater than the writing department, and that they have much to offer him, in the interpretation, the clarification, and illumination of what he has to say; and even if, sometimes, they wish him to express, or let him help them express, certain ideas and feelings of their own, he has now recognized that there are elements of the incomplete in his nature and in the work it produces. This is the third phase. There is some danger in it. There is the danger that the playwright may be as abruptly divested of confidence in his own convictions as that confidence was first born in him. He may suddenly become a sort of ventriloquist's dummy for ideas which are not his own at all. But that is a danger to which only the hack writer is exposed, and so it doesn't much matter. A serious playwright can only profit from passage into the third phase, for what he will now do is this: he will listen; he will consider; he will give a receptive attention to any creative mind that he has the good fortune to work with. His own mind, and its tastes, will open like the gates of a city no longer under siege. He will then be willing to supplement his personal conceptions with outside conceptions which he will have learned may be creative extensions of his own.

A mature playwright who has made this third and final step in his relations to fellow workers has come to accept the collaborative nature of the theater: he knows now that each artist in the theater is able to surpass his personal limits by respect for and acceptance of the talent and vision of others. When a gifted young actor rushes up to the playwright during rehearsals and cries out, I can't feel this, this doesn't ring true to me, the writer doesn't put on the austere mask of final authority. He moves over another seat from the aisle of a rehearsal hall, and bows his head in serious reflection while the actor tells him just what about the speech or the scene offends his sense of artistic justice, and usually the writer gets something from it. If he still disagrees with the actor, he says: "Let's get together with (whoever is directing) and talk this over at the bar next door. . . ." Maybe he won't sleep that night, but the chances are that in the morning he will reexamine the challenged segment with a sympathetic concern for an attitude which hasn't originated in his own brain and nerves, where sensibility is seated.

Now all of this that I've been rambling on about is my idea of the healthy course of development for a playwright *except*—I repeat, EXCEPT!—in those rare instances when the playwright's work is so highly individual that no one but the playwright is capable of discovering the right key for it.

When this rare instance occurs, the playwright has just two alternatives. Either he must stage his play himself or he must find one particular director who has the very unusual combination of a truly creative imagination plus a true longing, or even just a true willingness, to devote his own gifts to the faithful projection of someone else's vision. This is a thing of rarity. There are very few directors who are imaginative and yet also willing to forego the willful imposition of their own ideas on a play. How can you blame them? It is all but impossibly hard for any artist to devote his gifts to the mere interpretation of the gifts of another. He wants to leave his own special signature on whatever he works on.

Here we encounter the sadly familiar conflict between playwright and director. And just as a playwright must recognize the value of conceptions outside his own, a director of serious plays must learn to accept the fact that nobody knows a play better than the man who wrote it. The director must know that the playwright has already produced his play on the stage of his own imagination, and just as it is important for a playwright to forget certain vanities in the interest of the total creation of the stage, so must the director. I must observe that certain directors are somewhat too dedicated to the principle that all playwrights must be "corrected." I don't think a director should accept a directorial assignment without feeling that, basically, the author of the play, if it's a serious work by a playwright of ability, has earned and deserves the right to speak out, more or less freely, during the rehearsal and tryout period of the production if this can be done in a way that will not disturb the actors. Yet it sometimes happens that the playwright is made to feel a helpless bystander while his work is being prepared for Broadway. It seems to me that the director is privileged to tell the author to "Shut up!" actually or tacitly, only when it is unmistakably evident that he, the director, is in total artistic command of the situation. Sometimes a director will go immediately from one very challenging and exhausting play production into another, being already committed by contract to do so. Then naturally he can't bring the same vitality to the second that he brought to the first. This becomes evident when the play has been blocked out, and after this blocking, little further progress is being made. The play remains at the stage of its initial blocking. The director may say, and quite honestly feel, that what he is doing is giving the public and critics a play precisely as it was written. However, this is evading the need and obligation that I mentioned first in this article, that a play must nearly always be raised above its manuscript level by the creative gifts and energies of its director, and all others involved in its production.

Perhaps it would be a good idea, sometimes, to have a good psychiatrist in attendance at the rehearsals and tryout of a difficult play, one who is used to working with highly charged creative people such as directors and actors and playwrights and producers, so that whenever there is a collision of nervous, frightened, and defensive egos, he can arbitrate among them, analyze their personal problems which have caused their professional problems, and "smooth things over" through the clearing house of a wise and objective observer.

Once in a while the exigencies and pressures of Broadway

must step aside for another set of conditions which are too fragile and spiritually important to suffer violence through the silly but sadly human conflict of egos.

The theater *can* be a maker of great friendships!

If the Writing Is Honest

IF THE WRITING IS honest it cannot be separated from the
man who wrote it. It isn't so much his mirror as it is the dis-
tillation, the essence, of what is strongest and purest in his nature, whether that be gentleness or anger, serenity or torment,
light or dark. This makes it deeper than the surface likeness of
a mirror and that much more truthful.

I think the man William Inge is faithfully portrayed in
the work of William Inge the dramatist. The perceptive and
tender humanity that shines in *The Dark at the Top of the
Stairs* is a dominant trait of Bill Inge as I have known him
these past fourteen years. Now the American theater public
has begun to know him. When they enter The Music Box
theater of Forty-fifth Street, west of Broadway, it is like going
next door to call on a well-liked neighbor. There is warmth
and courtesy in their reception. There is an atmosphere of se-

This essay appeared in the *New York Times,* March 16, 1958. It is also
the preface to William Inge's *The Dark at the Top of the Stairs,* Random
House, 1958.

[100]

renity in his presence, there is understanding in it, and the kindness of wisdom and the wisdom of kindness. They enter and take comfortable seats by the fireside without anxiety, for there is no air of recent or incipient disorder on the premises. No bloodstained ax has been kicked under the sofa. If the lady of the house is absent, she has really gone to baby-sit for her sister, her corpse is not stuffed hastily back of the coal-bin. If the TV is turned on it will not break into the panicky report of unidentified aircraft of strange design over the roof-tops. In other words, they are given to believe that nothing at all disturbing or indecorous is going to happen to them in the course of their visit. But they are in for a surprise, not a violent one but a considerable one, for William Inge the playwright, like William Inge the gentleman from Kansas via St. Louis, uses his good manners for their proper dramatic purpose, which is to clothe a reality which is far from surface. It is done, as they say, with mirrors, but the mirrors may all of a sudden turn into X ray photos, and it is done so quietly and deftly that you hardly know the moment when the mirrors stop being mirrors and the more penetrating exposures begin to appear on the stage before you. All of a sudden, but without any startling explosion, it happens, and you're not sure just when and how. This nice, well-bred next door neighbor, with the accent that belongs to no region except the region of good manners, has begun to uncover a world within a world, and it is not the world that his welcome prepared you to meet, it's a secret world that exists behind the screen of neighborly decorum. And that's when and where you meet the talent of William Inge, the true and wonderful talent which is for offering, first, the genial surface of common American life, and then not ripping but quietly dropping the veil that keeps you from seeing yourself as you are. Somehow he does it in such a way that you are not offended or startled by it. It's just what you are, and why should you be ashamed of it? We are what we are, and why should we be ashamed of it more than enough to want to improve it a little? That's what Bill Inge tells you, in his quiet, gently modulated voice that belongs to no region but the region of sincerity and understanding. No, don't be ashamed of it, but see it and know it and make whatever corrections you feel able to make, and they are bound to be good ones.

X ray photos, coming out of mirrors, may reveal the ravages of tissues turning malignant or of arteries beginning to be obstructed by deposits of calcium or fat. This is God's or the devil's way of removing us to make room for our descendants. Do they work together, God and the devil? I sometimes suspect that there's a sort of understanding between them, which we won't understand until Doomsday.

But Inge reveals the operations of both these powerful mysteries in our lives if you will meet him halfway, and therein lies his very peculiar talent. You hardly know the revelation has happened until you have parted from him and started home, to your house next door to The Music Box on Forty-fifth Street.

This has a great deal to do with the fact that the very handsome and outwardly serene face of William Inge, the gentleman-playwright, looks a bit older than his forty years.

Take fourteen from forty-four years and you are left with thirty, which was Bill's age when I met him in St. Louis in January, 1945. This was just a few weeks after Laurette

Taylor had started breaking the ice of a Chicago winter with her performance, there, of my first success, *The Glass Menagerie*. I had returned to my parents' home in St. Louis as a refugee from the shock of sudden fame, but the flight was not far enough to serve its purpose. I had been home hardly a day when my mother interrupted my work in the basement of our rented suburban home—we had recently ascended from the city-apartment level of economy—to tell me the drama critic of the St. Louis *Star-Times* was on the phone. Bill Inge told me that he also did feature stories on theatrical folk passing through St. Louis and he would like to do a sort of "Home Town Boy Makes Good" article on me. He also wondered, sympathetically, if I would not enjoy a little social diversion other than that provided by family friends in St. Louis, since my own small group of past associates in the city had scattered far and wide, by this time, like fugitives from a sanguinary overthrow of state. He gave me his address and a time to come there. He was living in a housing project, way downtown in a raffish part of the city, but when he opened the door I saw over his shoulder a reproduction of my favorite Picasso and knew that the interview would be as painless as it turned out to be.

After I had gone back to Chicago to finish out the break-in run of *Menagerie*, Bill came up one weekend to see the play. I didn't know until then that Bill wanted to be a playwright. After the show, we walked back to my hotel in the Loop of Chicago, and on the way he suddenly confided to me, with characteristic simplicity and directness, that being a successful playwright was what he most wanted in the world for himself. This confession struck me, at the time, as being just a politeness, an effort to dispel the unreasonable gloom that had come over me at a time when I should have been most elated, an ominous letdown of spirit that followed me like my shadow wherever I went. I talked to him a little about this reaction, but I didn't feel that he was listening to me. I think Bill Inge had already made up his mind to invoke this same shadow and to suffuse it with light: and that, of course, is exactly what he has done.

The history of his rise in our theater is deceptively smooth in its surface appearance, for back of it lies the personal Odyssey of Bill Inge, and in the Odyssey, which I know and which has amazed and inspired me, is a drama as fine and admirable as any of the ones he has given, one after another—an unbroken succession of distinguished and successful plays—to the American theater, and someday I hope that he will make a play of it, his personal Iliad and Odyssey, a truly Homeric drama, but one in which the stairs rise from dark to light through something remarkably fine and gallant in his own nature.

Foreword to

Sweet Bird of Youth

WHEN I CAME to my writing desk on a recent morning, I found lying on my desk top an unmailed letter that I had written. I began reading it and found this sentence: "We are all civilized people, which means that we are all savages at heart but observing a few amenities of civilized behavior." Then I went on to say: "I am afraid that I observe fewer of these amenities than you do. Reason? My back is to the wall and has been to the wall for so long that the pressure of my back on the wall has started to crumble the plaster that covers the bricks and mortar."

Isn't it odd that I said the wall was giving way, not my back? I think so. Pursuing this course of free association, I suddenly remembered a dinner date I once had with a dis-

---

This foreword to the published version of *Sweet Bird of Youth,* New Directions, 1959, was written prior to the Broadway opening of the play and published in the *New York Times,* Sunday, March 8, 1959, under the headline "Williams' Wells of Violence."

tinguished colleague. During the course of this dinner, rather close to the end of it, he broke a long, mournful silence by lifting to me his sympathetic gaze and saying to me, sweetly, "Tennessee, don't you feel that you are blocked as a writer?"

I didn't stop to think of an answer, it came immediately off my tongue without any pause for planning. I said, "Oh, yes, I've always been blocked as a writer but my desire to write has been so strong that it has always broken down the block and gone past it."

Nothing untrue comes off the tongue that quickly. It is planned speeches that contain lies or dissimulations, not what you blurt out so spontaneously in one instant.

It was literally true. At the age of fourteen I discovered writing as an escape from a world of reality in which I felt acutely uncomfortable. It immediately became my place of retreat, my cave, my refuge. From what? From being called a sissy by the neighborhood kids, and Miss Nancy by my father, because I would rather read books in my grandfather's large and classical library than play marbles and baseball and other normal kid games, a result of a severe childhood illness and of excessive attachment to the female members of my family, who had coaxed me back into life.

I think no more than a week after I started writing I ran into the first block. It's hard to describe it in a way that will be understandable to anyone who is not a neurotic. I will try. All my life I have been haunted by the obsession that to desire a thing or to love a thing intensely is to place yourself in a vulnerable position, to be a possible, if not a probable, loser of what you most want. Let's leave it like that. That block has

always been there and always will be, and my chance of getting, or achieving, anything that I long for will always be
gravely reduced by the interminable existence of that block.

I described it once in a poem called "The Marvelous
Children."

"He, the demon, set up barricades of gold and purple tin-
foil, labeled Fear (and other august titles), which they, the
children, would leap lightly over, always tossing backwards
their wild laughter."

But having, always, to contend with this adversary of
fear, which was sometimes terror, gave me a certain tendency
toward an atmosphere of hysteria and violence in my writing,
an atmosphere that has existed in it since the beginning.

In my first published work, for which I received the big
sum of thirty-five dollars, a story published in the July or August issue of *Weird Tales* in the year 1928, I drew upon a
paragraph in the ancient histories of Herodotus to create a
story of how the Egyptian queen, Nitocris, invited all of her
enemies to a lavish banquet in a subterranean hall on the
shores of the Nile, and how, at the height of this banquet,
she excused herself from the table and opened sluice gates ad-
mitting the waters of the Nile into the locked banquet hall,
drowning her unloved guests like so many rats.

I was sixteen when I wrote this story, but already a con-
firmed writer, having entered upon this vocation at the age of
fourteen, and, if you're well acquainted with my writings
since then, I don't have to tell you that it set the keynote for
most of the work that has followed.

My first four plays, two of them performed in St. Louis,

were correspondingly violent or more so. My first play professionally produced and aimed at Broadway was *Battle of Angels* and it was about as violent as you can get on the stage.

During the nineteen years since then I have only produced five plays that are *not* violent: *The Glass Menagerie, You Touched Me, Summer and Smoke, The Rose Tattoo* and, recently in Florida, a serious comedy called *Period of Adjustment,* which is still being worked on.

What surprises me is the degree to which both critics and audience have accepted this barrage of violence. I think I was surprised, most of all, by the acceptance and praise of *Suddenly Last Summer.* When it was done off Broadway, I thought I would be critically tarred and feathered and ridden on a fence rail out of the New York theater, with no future haven except in translation for theaters abroad, who might mistakenly construe my work as a castigation of American morals, not understanding that I write about violence in American life only because I am not so well acquainted with the society of other countries.

Last year I thought it might help me as a writer to undertake psychoanalysis and so I did. The analyst, being acquainted with my work and recognizing the psychic wounds expressed in it, asked me, soon after we started, "Why are you so full of hate, anger, and envy?"

Hate was the word I contested. After much discussion and argument, we decided that "hate" was just a provisional term and that we would only use it till we had discovered the more precise term. But unfortunately I got restless and started hopping back and forth between the analyst's couch and some Caribbean beaches. I think before we called it quits I had persuaded the doctor that hate was not the right word, that there was some other thing, some other word for it, which we had not yet uncovered, and we left it like that.

Anger, oh yes! And envy, yes! But not hate. I think that hate is a thing, a feeling, that can only exist where there is no understanding. Significantly, good physicians never have it. They never hate their patients, no matter how hateful their patients may seem to be, with their relentless, maniacal concentration on their own tortured egos.

Since I am a member of the human race, when I attack its behavior toward fellow members I am obviously including myself in the attack, unless I regard myself as not human but superior to humanity. I don't. In fact, I can't expose a human weakness on the stage unless I know it through having it myself. I have exposed a good many human weaknesses and brutalities and consequently I have them.

I don't even think that I am more conscious of mine than any of you are of yours. Guilt is universal. I mean a strong sense of guilt. If there exists any area in which a man can rise above his moral condition, imposed upon him at birth and long before birth, by the nature of his breed, then I think it is only a willingness to know it, to face its existence in him, and I think that, at least below the conscious level, we all face it. Hence guilty feelings, and hence defiant aggressions, and hence the deep dark of despair that haunts our dreams, our creative work, and makes us distrust each other.

Enough of these philosophical abstractions, for now. To get back to writing for the theater, if there is any truth in the Aristotelian idea that violence is purged by its poetic representation on a stage, then it may be that my cycle of violent plays have had a moral justification after all. I know that I have felt it. I have always felt a release from the sense of meaninglessness and death when a work of tragic intention has seemed to me to have achieved that intention, even if only approximately, nearly.

I would say that there is something much bigger in life and death than we have become aware of (or adequately recorded) in our living and dying. And, further, to compound this shameless romanticism, I would say that our serious theater is a search for that something that is not yet successful but is still going on.

Reflections on a Revival of a Controversial Fantasy

IF THE PLAY, *Camino Real,* were a product being promoted on a TV commercial and I were the spokesman for it, I suppose I would present it in such theatrical terms as these:

"Are you more nervous and anxious than you want people to know?"

"Has your public smile come to resemble the grimace of a lion-tamer in a cage with a suddenly untamed lion, or that of a trapeze performer without a net beneath him and with a sudden attack of disequilibrium coming on him as he's about to perform his most hazardous trick near the top of the big top?"

"And do you have to continue your performance betraying no sign on your face of anxiety in your heart?"

"Then here is the right place for you, the Camino Real, its plaza and dried-up fountain, at the end of it. Here is where

This essay appeared in the *New York Times,* May 15, 1960.

you won't be lonely alone, bewildered alone, frightened alone, nor desperately brave alone, either."

Actually, there is a character in the play (she's called the Gypsy and she represents the wonderful, tough-skinned pedestrians of the Camino who were born and bred on it and wouldn't trade it for the Champs Élysées) who delivered a better pitch than mine, above, but hers doesn't precede the play, to introduce it.

I wrote this play in a time of desolation: I thought, as I'd thought often before and have often thought since, that my good work was done, that those "huge cloudy symbols of a high romance" that used to lift me up each morning (with the assistance of coffee so black you couldn't see through it even when you poured it before a fair-weather window), that all those mornings had gone like migratory birds that wouldn't fly back with any change of season. And so it was written to combat or to purify a despair that only another writer is likely to understand fully.

Despair is a thing that you can't live with anymore than you can live with a lover who hates you or a companion who never stops nagging. And even though it was my most spectacular and expensive failure on Broadway, *Camino Real* served for me, and I think for a number of others who saw it during its brief run in 1953, as a spiritual purgation of that abyss of confusion and lost sense of reality that I, and those others, had somehow wandered into.

There are two key speeches in the play, neither of which is more than one sentence. One is the remark of Don Quixote in the Prologue, when he arrives in the midnight plaza of this nowhere, everywhere place and hears all about him the whispering of the word "lonely" from beggar and outcast people asleep on the pavement. He seems oddly comforted by it: he turns to the audience and observes: "In a place where so many are lonely, it would be inexcusably selfish to be lonely alone."

The other key speech is at the end of the play, and is also only one sentence: "The violets in the mountains have broken the rocks." In the final, published version of *Camino Real*, both of these key speeches are given to Don Quixote, not because I regard him as a fool but because I think, and, yet, I do truly believe, that the human coat of arms can and must, finally, bear such romantic mottoes as these, at least in the later stretches of our Camino Reals.

What the play says through this unashamed old romanticist, Don Quixote, is just this, "Life is an unanswered question, but let's still believe in the dignity and importance of the question."

Tennessee Williams
Presents his POV

THE LAST TIME I was in Hollywood a famous lady columnist
with a way-out taste in millinery but a way-in taste in film fare
got me on the phone one morning and lit into me like a
mother tigress defending her litter. "I want to know why you
are always plunging into sewers!" she demanded.

I happened to like the lady and, as an avid reader of
movie fan magazines, I had derived many hours of pleasure
from her sometimes withering diatribes against stars whose
private behavior had offended her sense of propriety. So, I
did not shout back at her but tried to mollify her with a rea-
sonable dissertation on my artistic POV as opposed to hers
(and I will pause for one moment to say that POV is a handy
contraction of the term "point of view," which is used in the
shooting script of movie scenarios). I tried to persuade the
lady, in the gentlest possible manner, that from my POV it
was not into sewers but into the mainstream of life that I had

This essay appeared in the *New York Times Magazine,* June 12, 1960.

always descended for my material and characters. I did not succeed in altering her POV, but I did seem to calm her fury.

The POV of Miss Marya Mannes is essentially the same as Miss Hedda Hopper's POV, and even the POV of my mother, who says to me so often, "Son, when there is so much unpleasantness in the world, why is it necessary to put it on the stage?"

Mother's question was more sorrowful in tone than wrathful, but somehow that didn't make it any easier to answer, especially since even a middle-aged son still has a terrible sense of guilt in the presence of Mom. I'm not sure that I even tried to answer it, but one time, to my surprise, I heard her answer it for herself. A visitor was saying, "Mrs. Williams, why does your son waste his talents on such morbid subjects?"

Mother spoke as quickly as if she'd always known the answer. "My son," she said, "writes about life"—and she said it with the conviction of a rebel yell.

I am sorry to be speaking for and about my own work, in response to the POV of Miss Mannes, since I was not the solitary culprit she summoned to justice. My fellow defendants are Lillian Hellman, Albert Camus, Jean Genêt, and others, I would assume, such as Bertolt Brecht, Samuel Beckett, Jean Anouilh, Eugene Ionesco, Friedrich Duerrenmatt, and Edward Albee. It's a distinguished list and I am proud to be on it, and hopeful that my plea for the defense will not compromise them too much. I am hoping also that some among them will find an interval in their subversive creative activity to speak for themselves.

Let us begin with statistics. Immediately after reading the

piece by Miss Mannes, which would give the impression that virtually all Broadway houses this year had been preempted by works of violence, decadence and stomach-turning morbidity, I consulted the A. B. C. ads of theater attractions then running on Broadway, and I counted fifteen attractions in the musical and revue category.

Of the remaining nine attractions on Broadway, I found that only one or two might conceivably be subversive from the POV of Miss Mannes—that brilliantly witty import, Jean Giraudoux's *Duel of Angels,* and the prize-winning play by Lillian Hellman, *Toys in the Attic.*

The seven other legitimate attractions, although they do recognize with eloquence and dramatic skill that many circumstances in human existence are not as agreeable as all might wish for, could hardly be called "sick" plays, or even decadent, and all of them, from the humanistic POV, are distinctly affirmative. And so, on the basis of statistics, it appears to me that Miss Mannes is sounding a false alarm, or, at least, an alarm which is somewhat exaggerated.

Although she writes with a temperance which is unique among those sharing her POV, she is unmistakably out for blood, and the point I am making is that, quantitatively speaking, there isn't much blood to be out for, at least anywhere near Times Square; not enough to serve as a transfusion for an infant with a moderate thumb cut.

Now let's get down to my POV and that of my codefendants before a very formidable and ever more vocal tribunal. I dare to suggest, from my POV, that the theater has made in our time its greatest artistic advance through the unlocking and lighting up and ventilation of the closets, attics, and basements of human behavior and experience. Miss Hopper calls them "sewers"; so does Dorothy Kilgallen, and so, I'm afraid, at least by implication, does Miss Mannes. I think there has been not a very sick but a very healthy extension of the frontiers of theme and subject matter acceptable to our dramatic art, to the stage, the screen, and even television, despite the POV of "sponsors."

The POV I am speaking for is just this: that no significant area of human experience, and behavior reaction to it, should be held inaccessible, provided it is presented with honest intention and taste, to the screen, play, and TV writers of our desperate time. And I would add that to campaign against this advance in dramatic freedom is to campaign for something that is perilously close to a degree of cultural fascism, out of which came the Nazi book-burning and the "correction" of all the arts in the Russia of Stalin.

And, if you remember the statistics I noted earlier in this piece, you may agree with my POV that such a thing as this sort of cultural rigging is a greater peril than the so-called moral decadence of such works as *Caligula, The Threepenny Opera, The Visit, Toys in the Attic, The Zoo Story, Krapp's Last Tape, Camino Real,* and *The Connection,* most of which are pretty safely off Broadway.

The rallying cry of those who want our creative heads on the chopping block is: let's have plays affirming the essential dignity of mankind. It's a damned good platform. The only trouble with it, from my POV, is that we are not agreed about exactly what that high-sounding slogan really means in the way of truth about dignity and mankind.

People are humble and frightened and guilty at heart,

all of us, no matter how desperately we may try to appear otherwise. We have very little conviction of our essential decency, and consequently we are more interested in characters on the stage who share our hidden shames and fears, and we want the plays about us to say "I understand you. You and I are brothers; the deal is rugged but let's face and fight it together."

It is not the essential dignity but the essential ambiguity of man that I think needs to be stated.

Of course I am tempted to talk about my own characters —Blanche DuBois, Serafina delle Rose, and even the sick Princess Kosmonopolis—at this point, but let me have a bit of dignity and talk instead about Brecht's *Mother Courage,* the greatest of modern plays in my opinion.

Mother Courage was a jackal. She battened on the longest war in history, following the armies, in an ever increasingly beaten-up wagon, with her shoddy merchandise for which she extracted the highest price she could get. At one point she even denied that her son was her son, and let him be executed without an outcry except the awful outcry in her heart. Why? Because of her need to go on with her wagon and her demented daughter and her simple will to endure.

I have specified a work that I think affirms the only kind of essential human dignity and decency, in modern terms, that I can honestly swear by.

Miss Mannes only mentions *My Fair Lady,* and the others sharing her POV are curiously reluctant to provide us with a list of plays, classic or modern, especially modern, that conform to their moral specifications.

If you were Prince Hamlet and observed the suicidal

anguish of Ophelia, would you or would you not rise above all personal concerns, at least for a while, to embrace her kindly? Would you or would you not thrust a dagger through a curtain to kill a man behind it simply because you suspected, but surely weren't certain, that he might be your mother's lover and your father's killer?

From my POV I find Prince Hamlet cruel. How does he strike you from yours?

The magnitude of *Hamlet* does not exist in the matter but in the manner. Dramatic lyricism of the highest, most lasting order, and the passion to reveal the undignified and the often indecent truths about mankind are what make *Hamlet* so great a drama.

This is my POV, exemplified by one classic and one modern play.

The POV of Miss Mannes and company betrays a basic misapprehension of the creative nature and function.

There are two kinds of creative work: organic and non-organic. It is possible to reform, to change the nature of a non-organic (synthetic) work in the arts, meaning that work which is produced through something other than a necessity as built in to the worker as his heartbeat and respiration. But you could flay the skin off a writer whose work is organic and you still would not get out of him a sincere or workable recantation of his faith in what he is doing, however abominable that work may be or strike you as being.

The nervous system of any age or nation is its creative workers, its artists. And if that nervous system is profoundly disturbed by its environment, the work it produces will inescapably reflect the disturbance, sometimes obliquely and sometimes with violent directness, depending upon the nature and control of the artist.

I am giving away no trade secret when I point out how many artists, including writers, have sought refuge in psychiatry, alcohol, narcotics, way-in or way-out religious conversions, and so forth. An extension of the list would be boringly superfluous.

Deny the art of our time its only spring, which is the true expression of its passionately personal problems and their purification through work, and you will be left with a soil of such aridity that not even a cactus plant could flower upon it.

To sum it up for the defense: We have done no worse a deed than the X ray machine or the needle that makes the blood test. And though these are clinical devices, I think we have tried our best to indicate which are the healthy blood cells and which is the normal tissue in the world of our time, through exposing clearly the dark spots and the viruses on the plates and in the blood cultures.

Certainly, there should be a healthy coexistence of My Fair Lady and My Lady of Unwilling Sickness. But if one tries to push out the other, which is the fair one, really?

Prelude to a Comedy

PERHAPS NO OTHER occupation is more inclined to infiltrate and finally to absorb the life of the man engaged in it than the writer's calling.

In this context I recall having once written a preface to a poet friend's first volume of verse. The preface began something like this:

"In this time of false intensities, it is exhilarating to know the work of an artist which exists as a natural and joyful accompaniment to his life instead of almost being a substitute for it."

I believe, I went on to say, that I didn't think writing, nor any form of creative work, was ever meant by nature to be a man's way of making a living, that when it becomes one it almost certainly loses a measure of purity.

The first work of creative art was probably a caveman's

This essay appeared in the *New York Times,* November 6, 1960, just prior to the opening of *Period of Adjustment.*

drawing on the wall of his cave, and it wasn't done for fame or money or even the oh's and ah's of anyone but himself. I think he just picked up a sharp bit of stone and drew on the rock wall of his cave, the pure one-dimensional record in celebration of a bit of personal experience that had deeply moved him.

I suspect that it was the portrait of a dangerous wild beast he had encountered that day in the forest primeval—a beast that he had met in mortal combat and that he obviously had overcome and had, very likely, hauled home for supper. In fact, I suspect that maybe at the back of the cave his wife was broiling some good cuts of meat off the carcass, and it was by the light of her kitchen fire that this aboriginal artist carved with stone onto stone the record, the memorial of the event in the forest that day; an event that moved him to discover, for the first of all times on earth, the impulse of an artist to translate experience into something permanent.

I have seen photographs of these prehistoric rock carvings, which were the beginning of human history in art, and observed the beauty and dignity of them, and sensed the emotional turmoil of the earth's first artist, celebrating the dignity and beauty and valor of his victim even while its carcass was being prepared for supper.

I do wonder, however, if this first artist on earth was hungry enough to gnaw the bones of his conquered adversary with an appetite that wasn't reduced by the shame of devouring the flesh of the valiant victim.

I know he must have had pride in his victory over this slain adversary, but I also know that he must have been paying it homage when he carved its portrait on the cave wall by the light of the fire that prepared its flesh for supper.

What I meant in the opening remark of my preface to the poet's book was that his work had that kind of purity in it, that it had suffered no distortions in its descent from the first creative impulse and action of mankind.

I wrote this preface about twelve years ago, when I was myself a victim of the false intensities that seemed to follow on the transformation of a creative writer to a public figure, especially one who provides material for brilliantly satirical nightclub entertainers.

I felt this danger to the marrow of my bones, and I followed the instinctive reaction of running away. I cut out for Europe, and not one morning during the seven days of the crossing was I able to work with any degree of the joyfulness and naturalness that exhilarated me so much in my friend's first volume of verse.

A psychosomatic illness developed soon after my arrival in Paris and within ten days I was removed to the American hospital there. A coolly sympathetic young doctor told me that I was "threatened with hepatitis and mononucleosis."

These were a pair of disorders I had never heard of before and that had such formidable titles that I wrote in my diary, in my hospital room, "The jig is up: they have some fancy names for it."

Well, the jig wasn't up, I was simply suffering from an exaggerated form of that terrific shock of success that a youngish writer (I was thirty-six) is bound to experience when the privacy and natural joyfulness of his old way of working and living is intercepted like a forward pass in football by his abruptly turning into something less like a serious writer than the latest sensation of the entertainment world, where nothing is staler than the latest sensation a short while later.

Fortunately, I had made in Paris a friend, Mme. Lazareff, (the editor of the magazine *Elle*), who didn't take the dreadful names of the two disorders with which I was threatened as seriously as I did. She said to me, "Get dressed quick. I'm checking you out of here."

She not only checked me out of the hospital but also gave me the first dinner that I was able to keep down for a week and put me, that same evening, on a train to the South.

As Blanche said in *A Streetcar Named Desire;* "Sometimes there is God so quickly!"

In Rome there was sunlight and voices, human voices and the daybreak voices of those tiny swallows, which Italians call *ronzini,* thousands of them, swarming up and down at daybreak and dusk like great polka dot veils in a gale, reminding me of not only my lost mornings but my lost evenings, too, the naturalness and the joyfulness of them as they used to be.

I still believe that a writer's safety, especially in his middle years, if he began writing in his adolescence, lies in one of two things, whichever one is more personally suitable to him—living in a remote place, particularly on an island in the tropics, or in a fugitive way of life, running like a fox from place to place. I have tried both and am still trying both, but now I've found one other expedient, which is not to laugh at a problem but to stop taking it as if it affected the whole future course of the world. It surely doesn't: but to write intensely you have to believe intensely in what you're writing, at least for those few hours each day that you work.

One season in Rome I assayed the writing of a novella about the psychological adjustment of a famous actress to retirement from the stage. The actress encounters an old friend of considerable wisdom and candor, who says to her, "You can retire from a business but not from an art; you can't put your talent away like a key to a house where you don't live any more."

She spoke some true words there, and yet when the work of any kind of creative worker becomes tyrannically obsessive to the point of overshadowing his life, almost taking the place of it, he is in a hazardous situation. His situation is hazardous for the simple reason that the source, the fountainhead of his work, can only be his life.

No one ever used the material of his life so well as Marcel Proust, who made out of his life, recollected and continuing, what is possibly the greatest novel of our time, *The Remembrance of Things Past*, in which he made the passage of time (from past to present and to the future shadow) a controlled torrent of personal experience and sensibilities to it. It contains all the elements of a man's psychic history—his love, fear, loneliness, disgust, humor, and, most important of all, his forgiving perception of the reasons for the tragicomedy of human confusion.

The midnight dark of the final picture was irradiated and purified by a genius that no other writer of our century has in his command, not even Chekhov or Joyce. But within the limits of each, the writers of our times can use the method of Proust, that of transposing the contents of his life into a creative synthesis of it.

Only in this way can a writer justify his life and work and I think all serious writers know this and their serious audience has a sense of it, too.

Five Fiery Ladies

VIVIEN LEIGH IS not only the officially appointed first lady of the London theater, but several other things of equal or greater importance: an actress of great talent which has steadily grown through meeting the challenge of many classic roles, Greek, Shakespearean, Restoration, and Shaw, while still appearing so masterfully in such American films as *Gone With The Wind* and my own *Streetcar*. At present she is appearing in a film based on my novel, *The Roman Spring of Mrs. Stone,* a part she accepted with no reluctance despite its being an aging actress, retired from the stage and infatuated with a young adventurer more interested in mirrors than anything except money.

Her beauty, Vivien's, is as delicately flamboyant as an orchid. When she takes the stage, she commands it as if she first arrived there suspended from the bill of a stork.

Vivien, above all else, is incomparably graceful, she

This essay first appeared in *Life,* February 3, 1961.

moves like a marvelous dancer, on or off stage, and she has an instinct for doing and saying just the one right thing to put you at ease even when you know you are making a fool of yourself. All of these wonderful gifts she has given with no apparent regard for her personal vulnerability: in other words she is not only a stunning actress but a lady with the most important part of that intricate composition, which is kindness of heart.

Right now Geraldine Page is making her first motion picture in seven years, an extraordinarily long lapse of time between films for such a talented and beautiful actress. Her new film is a screen version of *Summer and Smoke* which she revived off Broadway for a year's run a good while after it expired so quickly on Broadway. This revival drew the attention of Hollywood to Gerry. But at that time Hollywood didn't know how to use her. She did not catch on with the picture public because of inept casting. Only in New York did her name continue to mean something, and there it meant something mostly to her own young generation of "method-trained" actors.

Some actresses have the kind of faces you can describe as "neutral." Their beauty must be created by magic, by suitable casting, by technical skill. It exists, but it has to be revealed. This was true of Garbo. She and Gerry have the same kind of beauty, great but unobtrusive until unveiled by some perceptive showman. Garbo had her great impresario, Stiller. Gerry had no one but Gerry. Did this throw her? Hell, no. She has spent the past seven years between her last picture and her new one on the study of her art. She is the most disciplined and dedicated of actresses, possibly the one that fate will select as an American Duse—provided that she continues to love the stage more than the screen. Last night when I called her long distance and inquired about her plans, she said, "I hope to find a new play for Broadway next fall."

MAGNANI! I put the name in caps with exclamation point because that is how she "comes on." She does not do it deliberately, and you can't explain it by the name and the legend. She is simply a rare being who seems to have about her a little lightning-shot cloud all her own that goes in and out with her as inescapably as her shadow. I think this explains her deep suffering from loneliness, her difficulty in human relations, her frequent pronouncement that she likes dogs better. In a crowded room, she can sit perfectly motionless and silent, and still you feel the atmospheric tension of her presence, its quiver and hum in the air like a live wire exposed, and a mood of Anna's is like the presence of royalty. Out of this phenomenon of human electronics has come the greatest acting art of our times. She can play a peasant or an empress, but Anna is haunted by a limitation that exists only in her mind. She feels advancing years may sometimes make her unsuitable for romantic roles. I say that her talent never rested on youth and never will.

Anna and I had both cherished the dream that her appearance in the part I created for her in *The Fugitive Kind* would be her greatest triumph to date, particularly since her co-star would be America's most gifted actor. But Mr. Brando comes at a high price in more ways than one, especially for a foreign co-player, still unsure of the language. Brando's offbeat timing and his slurred pronunciation were right for the part but they were torture for Anna who had to wait and wait for her cue, and when she received it, it would sometimes not be the one in the script. *The Fugitive Kind* is a true and beautiful film, in my opinion, but mutilated by that uncontrollable demon of competitiveness in an actor too great, if he knew it, to resort to such self-protective devices.

Kate is a playwright's dream actress. She makes dialogue sound better than it is by a matchless beauty and clarity of diction, and by a fineness of intelligence and sensibility that illuminates every shade of meaning in every line she speaks. She invests every scene, each "bit," with the intuition of an artist born into her art. Of the women stars that belong to a generation preceding that of "the method," Katharine Hepburn impresses me as having least needed that school of performance-in-depth. Like Laurette Taylor before her, she seems to do by instinct what years of "method" training have taught her juniors to do.

She is limited only by her ladylike voice and manner. Miss Hepburn could never play a tramp or a tenement housewife. No matter. There will always be parts for "ladies," and we need Kate Hepburn to play them.

I don't think Hepburn was happy with the part of the poet's mother in the screen version of *Suddenly Last Summer*. Brilliantly constructed as the screen version was by Gore Vidal, it still made unfortunate concessions to the realism that Hollywood is too often afraid to discard. And so a short morality play, in a lyrical style, was turned into a sensationally successful film that the public thinks was a literal study of such things as cannibalism, madness, and sexual deviation. But I am certain that Kate knew that what the drama truly concerned was all human confusion and its consequence: violence.

Liz Taylor is one of the great phenomena and symptoms of our time in America. Everything she has done with her life has been startling and sometimes implausible. It's hard to guess what Liz wants out of life: the million-dollar contracts and diamond necklaces or the exercise of what is probably the finest raw talent on the Hollywood screen. She has a deeply moving response to fellow artists in trouble, and so I'm inclined to believe that she is more interested in the creative work than the loot.

She thoroughly understands the system she is caught in, and she is not to be bossed or intimidated by it. Hollywood moguls have met their match in our Liz. I've heard her phone conversations with them: mutual understanding and respect. But what will emerge from this is something beyond my conjecture. Naturally I hope that this girl, this cross between a flower and the rock it sprang from, will discover that her greater satisfaction will come from the disciplining of her talent in the stricter conditions of our theater. But this is a personal bias and Liz Taylor, if luck is with her as it must be with us all, will probably wind up with insufficient space on wall or mantel for her big game trophies.

As for Liz's performance in *Suddenly Last Summer*, if it did nothing else, it demonstrated her ability to rise above miscasting. She was marvelously well cast as Maggie in *Cat on a Hot Tin Roof,* and that's when she should have got her

Oscar. But it stretched my credulity to believe that such a "hip" doll as our Liz wouldn't know at once in the film that she was "being used for something evil." I think that Liz would have dragged Sebastian home by his ears, and so saved them both from considerable embarrassment that summer.

Biography of
Carson McCullers

EVER SINCE A novelist told me that the theater was an art *manqué,* meaning something less than an art, and I got so mad that I nearly drove my car through the lowered gates of an Italian railroad crossing and smack into a *Rapido* from Naples to Rome, I have thought it best to limit my personal encounter with other writers almost as strictly as collisions should be limited between two speeding vehicles in any country. And yet somehow I have managed to make many close and deeply satisfying friendships with other writers, such as Paul and Jane Bowles, Gore Vidal, Truman Capote, Donald Windham, William Inge, Alberto Moravia, and, perhaps most of all, with Carson McCullers, despite the long periods in which we lived in very separate parts of the world. Let's face the fact that the almost constantly irritated sensibilities of writers make it difficult for them to get along together

This essay appeared in the *Saturday Review of Literature*, September 23, 1961.

as well as they should. This is especially true between novelists and playwrights. Novelists have the idea that playwrights are the pecuniary favorites of fortune, and they have some justification in this suspicion. Novelists and poets seem to be expected to live on air and subsidies, usually meager, while it is embarrassingly true that playwrights are recipients of comparatively large royalties, have Diners' Club cards, eat at Sardi's, and can travel first class. And so, on the surface, which is always misleading, they appear to be the favorites of fortune, and it is quite understandable and forgivable that their poet and novelist friends are tempted to goad them about the impurities of their medium.

Yet when this invidious attitude is dispelled, it can be agreeable for them to get together. The playwright must put aside his envy of the poet's or novelist's connection with a purer medium, and the novelist or the poet must have the good sense and sensibility to see that the material advantages of the playwright are incidental.

Carson McCullers and I have never had this embarrassment between us, although she is more consistently a writer of fiction than a playwright. From the moment of our first meeting, Carson, with her phenomenal understanding of another vulnerable being, felt nothing for me but that affectionate compassion that I needed so much and that she can give so freely, more freely than anyone else I know in the world of letters.

On the island of Nantucket, the summer of 1946, we worked at opposite ends of a table, she on a dramatization of *The Member of the Wedding* and I on *Summer and Smoke*, and for the first time I found it completely comfortable to work in the same room with another writer. We read each other our day's work over our after-dinner drinks, and she gave me the heart to continue a play that I feared was hopeless.

When I told her that I thought my creative powers were exhausted, she said to me, wisely and truly, an artist always feels that dread, that terror, when he has completed a work to which his heart has been so totally committed that the finishing of it seems to have finished him too, that what he lives for is gone like yesteryear's snow.

At the end of that summer's work I became very ill, and only a few months later so did she, with a mysterious paralysis of her right arm. I have such a fierce resistance to physical illness that I continually push it back; Carson's strength is enormous but primarily exists in her spirit. From 1947 to the present year she has been, as many interested in American writing know, a gallant invalid. She has lived with that paralysis of the right arm and with an excruciating series of operations to correct it, yet all the while she has never surrendered to it. During those fourteen years she has kept on working steadily and with all the creative and personal distinction that makes her an inspiring figure to us relative weaklings. She has completed two plays of the most impressive quality, and at the same time she has given us stories and poems of the purest distinction.

And all this time, these fourteen years, she has also been working on her fifth novel, *Clock Without Hands*.

Before I went abroad last spring, she told me that she felt she couldn't complete it, that she had paid out all her strength. Then I reminded her of what she had told me, those fourteen years ago, that at the end, or near it, of a work to which the artist's heart is totally committed, he always feels that dread, that terror which is greater than the fear of death.

When I returned from abroad, two and a half months later, an advance copy of the completed novel was waiting for me in Key West.

If I hadn't known before that Carson is a worker of miracles, this work would surely have convinced me of it, for without any sign of the dreadful circumstances under which she accomplished it, this work was once again a thing set on paper as indelibly as if it had been carved onto stone. Here was all the stature, nobility of spirit, and profound understanding of the lonely, searching heart that make her, in my opinion, the greatest living writer of our country, if not of the world.

A Summer of Discovery

IN THOSE DAYS there was, and for all I know still may be, a share-the-expense travel agency through which people whose funds were as limited as mine, that summer of 1940, go into contact with others who owned cars and were going in roughly the same direction.

A preliminary meeting and interview would be arranged in the office of the agency which was located in the lobby of a rather seedy midtown Manhattan hotel. It was about as embarrassing as applying for a job, perhaps even more so, for a man who is offering you a job can turn you down with some polite little dissimulation such as, "I'm looking for someone with a bit more experience in this type of work." But if you were turned down by a car-owner at this agency, you knew it could only be because you had failed to make an

---

This essay appeared in the *New York Herald Tribune*, Sunday, December 24, 1961, just prior to the Broadway opening of *The Night of the Iguana*.

agreeable or trustworthy impression. Inevitably you were nervous and guilty-looking.

On this occasion, the summer that I had decided to go to Mexico for no more definite reason than that it was as far from New York as I could hope to get on the small funds at my disposal, the agency introduced me to a fantastic young honeymoon couple. The bridegroom was a young Mexican who had come up to New York to visit the World's Fair, then in progress, and had encountered and almost immediately married a young blonde lady of ambiguous profession whom he was now preparing to take home to meet his parents in Mexico City.

He had already met with so many unexpected expenses that he needed a paying passenger on his trip home, but it was obvious that my nervous manner aroused suspicion in him. Fortunately they had an interpreter with them, at the meeting, and the bride was more accustomed to and less distrustful of nervous young men. She felt nothing at all alarming about me, and through the interpreter persuaded her bridegroom to accept me as a travelling companion.

They didn't speak the same language in more ways than one and so the young lady, as the journey proceeded, began to use me as her confidant. About her ambiguous profession she had thoroughly deceived her new mate but she was very uncertain that his well-to-do parents in Mexico City, if we ever got there, would be equally gullible. And so, on the long way South, she would rap at my motel door almost every midnight to tell me about their latest misunderstanding or misadventure, and these clandestine conversations were the best psychological therapy that I could have had in my own state of anxiety and emotional turmoil, which was due to my feeling that my career as a Broadway playwright had stopped almost where it had started and what would follow was unpredictable but surely no good.

The journey was erratic as a blind bird's and took at least twice as long as would be reasonably expected, and the shared expenses were staggering by my standards. However my state of mind and emotion were so depressed that I was fairly indifferent to all practical concerns, even to a bad cold that turned to influenza, to the almost continual dream-state that comes with high fever and chills.

I never again saw this odd young couple after the morning when they delivered me to the YMCA building in Mexico City but, a year or two later, the bride sent me some fairly worthless articles of clothing which I had left in the trunk of the car, along with a note containing sentimental references to the wonderful trip that we had enjoyed together and hoping that sometime, somehow, we'd be able to enjoy another, and I thought to myself as I read it, this poor young woman has gone out of her mind.

Nobody had warned me that Mexico City was, in altitude, one of the highest cities in the world. I felt all the time as if I had taken Benzedrine, couldn't sleep, couldn't stay still. Surmising at last that I was allergic to atmosphere at the 7,500-foot level, I took a bus to Acapulco, some other young American having described it as a primitive place with much better swimming facilities than the "Y".

So I set out for Acapulco, with chills, fever, heart palpitations, and a mental state that was like a somnambulist's, apparently not bothering to inform Audrey Wood, my agent, the Theatre Guild, or the Dramatist's Guild that my address would no longer be c/o General Delivery in Mexico City, an oversight which led to much complication some weeks later. Actually I was suffering from incipient tuberculosis, the scars of which are still visible on X ray lung photos.

In Acapulco, I spent the first few days in a fantastic hotel near the central plaza. All the rooms opened onto a large patio-garden containing parrots, monkeys, and the proprietor of the hotel, who was so fat that he could hardly squeeze into a room at the place. Much of his time was devoted to cosmetic treatments which were administered in the patio. Every morning a very lively young barber would arrive to touch up the proprietor's hair with henna and give him a marcel wave and a cold cream facial. Since the dyed, waved hair was quite long and the proprietor spoke in a falsetto voice and was always clad in a bright silk kimono, I wasn't quite sure of his sex till I heard him addressed as Señor something-or-other by one of his employees.

The steaming hot squalor of that place quickly drove me to look for other accommodations, nearer the beaches. And that's how I discovered the background for my new play, *The Night of the Iguana*. I found a frame hotel called the Costa Verde on the hill over the still water beach called Caleta and stayed there from late August to late September.

It was a desperate period in my life, but it's during such times that we are most alive and they are the times that we remember most vividly, and a writer draws out of vivid and desperate intervals in his life the most necessary impulse or drive toward his work, which is the transmutation of experience into some significant piece of creation, just as an oyster transforms, or covers over, the irritating grain of sand in his shell to a pearl, white or black, of lesser or greater value.

My daily program at the Costa Verde Hotel was the same as it had been everywhere else. I charged my nerves with strong black coffee, then went to my portable typewriter which was set on a card table on a veranda and worked till I was exhausted: then I ran down the hill to the still water beach for my swim.

One morning, taking my swim, I had a particularly bad fit of coughing. I tasted in my mouth something saltier than the waters of the Pacific and noticed beside my head, flowing from my mouth, a thin but bright thread of red blood. It was startling but not frightening to me, in fact I kept on swimming toward the opposite side of the bay, hardly bothering to look back to see if the trajectory of coughed-up blood was still trailing behind me, this being the summer when the prospect of death was hardly important to me.

What was important to me was the dreamworld of a new play. I have a theory that an artist will never die or go mad while he is engaged in a piece of work that is very important to him. All the cells of his body, all of his vital organs, as well as the brain cells in which volition is seated, seem to combine their forces to keep him alive and in control of his faculties. He may act crazily but he isn't crazy; he may show any symptom of mortality but he isn't dying.

As the world of reality in which I was caught began to dim out, as the work on the play continued, so did the death wish and the symptoms of it. And I remember this summer as the one when I got along best with people and when they seemed to like me, and I would attribute this condition to

[141]

the fact that I expected to be dead before the summer was over and that there was consequently no reason for me to worry about what people thought of me. When you stop worrying what people think of you, you suddenly find yourself thinking of them, not yourself, and then, for the time that this condition remains, you have a sort of crazy charm for chance acquaintances such as the ones that were staying with me that crazy summer of 1940, at the Costa Verde in Acapulco.

By the middle of September the bleeding lungs had stopped bleeding, and the death wish had gone, and has never come back to me since. The only mementos of the summer are the scar on the X ray plate, a story called "The Night of the Iguana," and now this play which has very little relation to the story except the same title and a bit of the same symbolism. But in both the short story and the play, written many years later, there is an incident of the capture of the iguana, which is a type of lizard, and its tying up under the veranda floor of the Costa Verde, which no longer exists in the new Acapulco.

Some critics resent my symbols, but let me ask, what would I do without them? Without my symbols I might still be employed by the International Shoe Co. in St. Louis.

Let me go further and say that unless the events of a life are translated into significant meanings, then life holds no more revelation than death, and possibly even less.

In September, that summer of 1940, the summer when, sick to death of myself, I turned to other people most truly, I discovered a human heart as troubled as my own. It was that of another young writer, a writer of magazine fiction who had just arrived from Tahiti because he feared that the war, which was then at a climax of fury, might cut him off from the magazines that purchased his adventure stories. But in Tahiti he had found that place which all of us spend our lives looking for, the one right home of the heart, and as the summer wore on I discovered that his desolation was greater than my own, since he was so despondent that he could no longer work.

There were hammocks along the sleeping verandas. We would spend the evenings in adjacent hammocks, drinking rum-cocos, and discussing and comparing our respective heartbreaks, more and more peacefully as the night advanced.

It was an equinoctial season, and every night or so there would be a spectacular storm. I have never heard such thunder or seen such lightning except in melodramatic performances of Shakespeare. All of the inarticulate but passionate fury of the physical universe would sometimes be hurled at the hilltop and the veranda, and we were thrilled by it, it would completely eclipse our melancholy.

But the equinox wore itself out by late September, and we both returned to our gloomy introspections.

Day after steaming hot day I would go to Wells Fargo in town for my option check and it wouldn't be there. It was long overdue and I was living on credit at the hotel, and I noticed, or suspected, a steady increase in the management's distrust of me.

I assumed that the Theatre Guild had dropped their option of *Battle of Angels* and lost all interest in me. The other young writer, still unable to scribble a line that he didn't scratch out with the groan of a dying beast, had no encouragement for me. He felt that it was quite clear that we had both arrived at the end of our ropes and that we'd better face it. We were both approaching the age of thirty, and he declared that we were not meant by implacable nature to go past that milestone, that it was the dead end for us.

Our gloom was not relieved by the presence of a party of German Nazis who were ecstatic over the early successes of the Luftwaffe over the R.A.F. When they were not gamboling euphorically on the beach, they were listening to the radio reports on the battle for Britain and their imminent conquest of it, and the entire democratic world.

My writer friend began to deliver a pitch for suicide as the only decent and dignified way out for either of us. I disagreed with him, but very mildly.

Then one day the manager of the hotel told me that my credit had run out. I would have to leave the next morning, so that night my friend and I had more than our usual quota of rum-cocos, a drink that is prepared in a cocoanut shell by chopping off one end of it with a machete and mixing the juice of the nut with variable quantities of rum, a bit of lemon juice, a bit of sugar, and some cracked ice. You stick straws in the lopped-off end of the cocoanut and it's a long dreamy drink, the most delectable summer night's drink I've ever enjoyed, and that night we lay in our hammocks and had rum-cocos until the stars of the Southern Cross, which was visible in the sky from our veranda, began to flit crazily about like fireflies caught in a bottle.

My friend reverted to the subject of death as a preferable alternative to life and was more than usually eloquent on the subject. It would have been logical for me to accept his argument but something in me resisted. He said I was just being "chicken," that if I had any guts I would go down the hill with him, right then and now, and take "the long swim to China," as I was no more endurably situated on earth than he was.

All that I had, he told me, was the uncontrolled emotionalism of a minor lyric talent which was totally unsuited to the stage of life as well as the theater stage. I was, he said, a cotton-headed romanticist, a hopeless anachronism in the world now lit by super fire-bombs. He reeled out of his hammock and to the veranda steps, shouting, "Come on, you chicken, we're going to swim out to China!"

But I stayed in my hammock, and if he went swimming that night, it wasn't to China, for when I woke up in the hammock, and it was daylight, he was dressed and packed and had found an elderly tourist who had a car and was driving back to Texas, and had invited us to accompany him in his car free of charge. My friend hauled me out of the hammock and helped me pack for departure.

This old man, he declared, referring to our driver, is in the same boat as we are, and the best thing that could happen to all three of us is to miss a turn through the mountains and plunge off the road down a chasm, to everlasting oblivion. On this note, we cut out.

We had just reached the most hazardous section of the narrow road through the mountains when this other young writer asked the tourist if he couldn't take over the wheel for a while. Oh, no, I exclaimed. But the other writer insisted, and like a bat out of hell he took those hairpin turns through the Sierras. Any moment, I thought, we would surely crash into the mountain or plunge into the chasm on the road's

[145]

other side, and it was then that I was all through with my death wish and knew that it was life that I longed for, on any terms that were offered.

I clenched my hands, bit my tongue, and kept praying. And gradually the driver's demonic spirit wore itself out, the car slowed, and he turned the wheel over to the owner and retired to the back seat to sleep off his aborted flirtation with the dark angel.

The Night of the Iguana is rooted in the atmosphere and experiences of the summer of 1940, which I remember more vividly, on the emotional level, than any summer that I have gone through before or after—since it was then, that summer, that I not only discovered that it was life that I truly longed for, but that all which is most valuable in life is escaping from the narrow cubicle of one's self to a sort of veranda between the sky and the still water beach (allegorically speaking) and to a hammock beside another beleaguered being, someone else who is in exile from the place and time of his heart's fulfillment.

A play that is more of a dramatic poem than a play is bound to rest on metaphorical ways of expression. Symbols and their meanings must be arrived at through a period of time which is often a long one, requiring much patience, but if you wait out this period of time, if you permit it to clear as naturally as a sky after a storm, it will reward you, finally, with a puzzle which is still puzzling but which, whether you fathom it or not, still has the beautifully disturbing sense of truth, as much of that ambiguous quality as we are permitted to know in all our seasons and travels and places of short stay on this risky planet.

At one point in the composition of this work it had an alternative title, *Two Acts of Grace,* a title which referred to a pair of desperate people who had the humble nobility of each putting the other's desperation, during the course of a night, above his concern for his own.

Being an unregenerate romanticist, even now, I can still think of nothing that gives more meaning to living.

T. Williams's View of T. Bankhead

I HAVE BEEN invited to contribute to these pages an explication of the meaning and history of my latest version of my "last long play for Broadway," but I am sure you will forgive me for hoping that the play will speak for itself, and to choose the relevant subject of Miss Tallulah Bankhead.

Shall I begin by speaking of her position in her profession, which she says that she hates?

Well, she isn't a Method actress and she is no more a member of the New Wave of theater personalities than I am. We are both veteran performers in our respective departments of the English-speaking theater. And if I should say that I hated writing plays it would be as reliable a statement as Tallulah's statement that she hates the theater.

She loves it with so much of her heart that, in order to protect her heart, she has to say that she hates it. But we

This essay appeared in the *New York Times*, December 29, 1963.

know better when we see her onstage. Of course she doesn't know better. The last thing she could ever be, at all consciously, is a liar, despite the fact that she has worked forty years in a world where the Eleventh Commandment often seems to be "Never speak the truth."

Tallulah has never hesitated to speak what she feels to be the truth, no matter about the possible hurt to herself, because when you speak the truth it is you, the speaker, who is most apt to be hurt.

Tallulah is the strongest of all the hurt people I've ever known in my life. And of hurt people I've known a remarkable number, including some whom I have hurt myself, and one of them is Tallulah.

She has forgiven me for it but I am not yet ready to forgive myself.

There is a peculiar sort of consanguinity of spirit between Tallulah and me, despite the fact that she is descended from the plantation Southland and I am descended, on my father's side, from Southern folk who owned no plantations because there are no plantations in the hills of East Tennessee.

We are closely linked in the way of understanding each other to such an extent that we can say anything that we want to say to each other, as long as we say it honestly, without there resulting anything but a bit of temporary glowering between us which leads to more understanding.

Tallulah says to me: "Every good female part you've ever written you've written for *me!*" Tallulah is more than slightly right about that, despite the fact that I have written only four parts for her, Myra Torrance in *Battle of Angels,* Blanche in *A Streetcar Named Desire,* The Princess Kosmonopolis in

Sweet Bird of Youth, and now, finally, Flora Goforth in *The Milk Train.*

Of these four roles that were written for Tallulah, she has chosen to perform only two, including the one in which you will have a chance to see her on Wednesday.

This intense infatuation of mine began in the summer of 1940. I happened to be in Provincetown, Mass., when Tallulah began an engagement at a playhouse halfway down the Cape. I rode a bicycle down there to see her because she was one of a list to whom the Theatre Guild had submitted my first play bought for Broadway. It so happened that the trip was longer than I had expected and it also so happened that as I was parking the bicycle on the Playhouse lawn, I heard someone calling out, "Five minutes, Miss Bankhead."

There was a response to the call, and this response was delivered in a voice that, having once heard, I would never stop hearing inside my head as I wrote lines for ladies that had somehow resulted from the fantastic crossbreeding of a moth and a tiger. Here was the voice for which I had written the part of Myra Torrance in *Battle of Angels,* and written it for that voice without ever having heard it except in films.

I went backstage after the play that night and she received me in her dressing room with that graciousness that has nothing to do with her Southern origin and genteel breeding but with her instinctive kindness to a person in whom she senses a vulnerability that is kin to her own. I suppose I simply mean that she saw or sensed immediately that I was meeting, for the first time in my life, a great star, and that I was more than just properly awed. I was virtually dumbstruck. I can't quote accurately the conversation between us. I think she asked who I was and then I think she said something like, "Oh, so it's you, the play is impossible, darling, but sit down and have a drink with me."

Which I did.

After a few moments she saw that her rejection of the play had struck me where I lived, and being by nature a person as kind as she is honest, she began to say more about it. Naturally, I can't quote her literally, these twenty-three years later, but I know that she did tell me that she sensed a sort of poetry in the play that was struggling toward theatrical viability but had not arrived there yet. And I know that her sweetness so moved me that the ride back up the Cape was more like floating on a cloud than pedaling a bicycle.

A year or so later this play I'd tried to sell her had failed spectacularly in Boston and I had so declined in favor and fortune that I was passing a month of the winter in the unheated attic of the family home in St. Louis. It was in that city that I next encountered Miss Bankhead. She was storming across the country as the maleficent vixen in *The Little Foxes*. I presented myself once more at her dressing room door and she received me as if she'd last seen me the day before yesterday, not the year before the last. "Well, darling," she roared, "I was luckier than Miriam Hopkins who lost her mind and actually appeared in that abominable Battle of Something that you had the impertinence to write for me!"

Now let's get on the *Streetcar*. It is the winter of 1946–1947 and as always while writing a play very close to my heart, I think I am dying. My worktable is beneath a New

Orleans skylight and beside it is the spectral figure of a lady and a star, impatiently keeping watch over my last agony at the typewriter. She is not still for a moment. She is sweeping all about me as I work, crying out, laughing, sobbing, but never losing the arrogance of a lady descended from a queen of Scotland. It is duly submitted to my agent, Audrey Wood, and after a short time that seemed like a century to me, Miss Wood dispatches a wire, mysteriously summoning me to a conference in Charleston, S.C.

In the wire she mentioned that I would there be introduced to a person so important as to be called a personage, and since I have always been hooked on mystery and importance, I pulled my dying body together and caught a plane to the designated place of top-level consultation.

The personage was a lady whose father was a Hollywood monarch and whose husband was another.

"Whom do you have in mind," asked this lady-producer, "for your fantastic Blanche?"

"Well," said I, "while I was writing this play, all of the speeches seemed to be issuing from the mouth of Miss Bankhead."

The lady-producer said that she admired that inimitable voice as much as I did but that she feared that Tallulah would have such power in the part of Blanche that, if she consented to play it, the moth-like side of Blanche would be demolished at once by the tiger-like side of Blanche. And I must shamefully admit that, being a "dying man," I lacked the strength to oppose this strongly stated opinion, being not only a man who thought he was dying but a playwright who had entered that phase of a playwright's remorseless cycle of existence when he may even suspect that unanimous "Yes" notices can add up to a sweetly disguised obituary to his professional being.

The Tiger-Moth called Blanche was superbly played by such stars as Jessica Tandy and Uta Hagen before that part and Tallulah got together, under circumstances that probably only Tallulah Bankhead would have the quixotic valor to confront without fear, or any evidence of it.

I have no wound-up watch and no looked-at calendar and such a dread of time passing, and past, that I can't tell you the year when Tallulah played Blanche; but play it she finally did, and with that Tiger-Moth quality of the lady and star who had haunted the sky-lit workroom in which I had caught Blanche DuBois in the paper facsimile of a jungle trap.

Some people who saw Tallulah's interpretation of Blanche have mistakenly said that she was too strong for the part of this neurasthenic creature, but I personally feel that she gave a magnificent portrayal of the role. I don't suppose anyone reads *Streetcar* anymore, but if they did, they would discover that Blanche is a delicate tigress with her back to the wall. The part must be played opposite an actor of towering presence, a Brando or a Tony Quinn, to create a plausible balance, but circumstances necessitated her playing it opposite an actor who would appear to best advantage as the male lead of a gently poetic play such as, say, something by Chekhov, Synge, or Yeats. And he made Tallulah's incandescent Blanche seem a bit too incandescent.

And now I want to tell you something about Tallulah that I think may convince you that the legend of great Southern ladies is not a myth.

No one could play the part of Flora Goforth in *The Milk Train* with the idea that being selected for the role was exactly a compliment to her, except as an actress of remarkable power.

Well, it's no secret that the play was presented last season on Broadway during the newspaper blackout and ran for only sixty-nine performances and cost its producers, including myself, a pretty tidy sum.

Now here is the lovely story about Tallulah and this play.

One evening before the production my phone rang in Key West.

"Tennessee, darling, I have read your new play and I would like to play it."

My answer? It was an occasion when I might have lied if I had time to think of a lie, believe me, but there was only time to either hang up the phone or speak the truth.

So I said: "Tallulah, I wrote it for you but it wasn't ready for you, so I tried it out in Spoleto with an English actress, Hermione Baddeley, and she was so terrific that I staggered into her dressing room, after the Spoleto opening, and said, 'Hermione, this play will be yours if you want it next season on Broadway.'"

What did Tallulah say? She said: "Well, darling, you did the right thing and that's that. But if it doesn't work because it isn't ready, well, you know me. And I know you wrote it for me and sometime I'm going to play it."

Well, it wasn't ready but now maybe it is, and though I have before me only a Coke laced with a bit of vodka instead of the finest champagne, I raise the glass to drink a toast to Tallulah, lady and star.

Too Personal?

THE GREATEST DANGER, professionally, of becoming the subject of so many "write-ups" and personal appearances on TV and lecture platforms is that the materials of your life, which are, in the case of all organic writing, the materials of your work, are sort of telegraphed in to those who see you and to those who read about you. So, when you get to the serious organization of this material into your work, people (meaning audiences and critics—all but the few most tolerant whom you naturally regard as the best) have a sort of *dèjá vu or déjà entendu* reaction to these materials which you have submitted to the cathartic process of your "sullen craft and art."

You may justifiably wonder why a man of my years in his profession, recognizing this hazard, has yet been willing to expose himself (with a frequency which seems almost

---

Tennessee Williams notes that this essay was to be a preopening piece in the *New York Times*, but they chose to interview him instead. It is now included as an introduction to *Small Craft Warnings*, New Directions, 1972.

symptomatic of clinical exhibitionism) to all of these interviews and the fewer, but equally personal, exposures on platform and "the tube."

I can offer you at least two reasons for this phenomenon.
One is probably something with which you will immediately
empathize. When one has passed through an extensive period
of that excess of privacy which is imposed upon a person
drifting almost willfully out of contact with the world, antici-
pating that final seclusion of the nonbeing, there comes upon
him, when that period wears itself out and he is still alive, an
almost insatiable hunger for recognition of the fact that he is,
indeed, still alive, both as a man and artist. That's reason
number one. The other is rather comical, I'm afraid. You get
a devastatingly bad write-up, and you feel that you are
washed up for good. Then some magazine editor gets through
to you on that phone in the studio of your tropical retreat, the
phone that you never pick up till it's rung so persistently that
you assume that your secretary and house guests have been
immobilized by nerve gas or something of that nature, and this
editor speaks to you as sympathetically as the family doctor
to a child stricken with a perforated appendix and tells you
that he is as shocked as you were by the tasteless exposé-type
of interview which appeared about you in a recent issue of
some other mag. And then, of course, you forget about work,
and you rage yourself into a slather over the iniquities and
duplicities of the "interviewer" referred to. You say, "Why,
that creature was so drunk he didn't know what street I lived
on, and the guy that set me up for him laced my martini with
sodium Pentothal, and all I remember about this occasion is
that my head came off my shoulders and his the ceiling and

I heard myself babbling away like an hysteric and I hadn't the slightest notion that he had a concealed tape recorder with him, and later he offered to play bridge with me that night, and he came over again with the tape recorder in some orifice of his body, I presume, and you know I do not see well and you know I like to hold forth to apparently amiable listeners, and I just assume that when they say 'I am interested only in your work,' that that's what they mean."

Now the editor has you on the hook.

"That's exactly my reaction to the revolting piece and how about letting us do a piece to correct it?"

You grasp at this offer like a drowning rat climbs on to anything that will float it. So you get another write-up. Then after this write-up, which is usually more colorful and better written than the one before, but equally nonserious, if not downright clownish, you feel that it is a life-or-death matter, professionally, with a new play opening somewhere, to correct the hilarious misquotes and exaggerations which embellished the second write-up, and so you go on to others and others. Now at last you have poured out, compulsively and perhaps fatally, all the recent content of your experience which should have been held in reserve for its proper place, which is in the work you're doing every morning (which, in my case, is the writing I do an hour or so before daybreak).

Is it or is it not right or wrong for a playwright to put his persona into his work?

My answer is: "What else can he do?"—I mean the very root-necessity of all creative work is to express those things most involved in one's particular experience. Otherwise, is the work, however well executed, not a manufactured, a synthetic thing? I've said, perhaps repeatedly, that I have two major classifications for writing: that which is organic and that which is not. And this opinion still holds.

Now let me attempt to entertain you once more with an anecdote.

Long ago, in the early forties, I attended a very posh party given by the Theatre Guild. I was comfortably and happily seated at a small table with my dear friend Miss Jo Healy, who was receptionist at the Guild in those days, when a lady with eyes that blazed with some nameless frenzy rushed up to me like a guided missile and seized me by the arm and shrieked to me, "You've got to meet Miss Ferber, she's dying to meet you."

Now in those days I was at least pliable, and so I permitted myself to be hauled over to a large table at which were seated a number of Diamond T trucks disguised as ladies.

"Oh, Miss Ferber," shrieked my unknown pilot, "this is Tennessee Williams."

Miss Ferber gazed slowly up and delivered this annihilating one-liner:

"The best I can manage is a mild 'Yippee.' "

"Madam," I said, "I can't even manage that."

Now everyone knows, who is cognizant of the world of letters, that Miss Edna Ferber was a creature of mammoth productivity and success. She was good at doing her thing; her novel and picture sales are fairly astronomical, I would guess.

I bring her up because she represents to me the classic, the archetypal, example of a writer whose work is impersonal, at least upon any recognizable level. I cannot see her in the oil fields of Texas with Rock Hudson and the late James Dean. Nor can I see her in any of her other impressive epics. I see her only as a lady who chose to put down a writer who was then young and vulnerable with such a gratuitously malicious one-liner. I mean without provocation, since I had literally been dragged to the steps of her throne.

So far I have spoken only in defense of the personal kind of writing. Now I assure you that I know it can be overdone. It is the responsibility of the writer to put his experience as a being into work that refines it and elevates it and that makes of it an essence that a wide audience can somehow manage to feel in themselves: "This is true."

In all human experience, there are parallels which permit common understanding in the telling and hearing, and it is the frightening responsibility of an artist to make what is directly or allusively close to his own being communicable and understandable, however disturbingly, to the hearts and minds of all whom he addresses.

Homage to Key West

MY ATTACHMENT TO the island of Key West dates back to 1941 when I sought solace there from the first important disaster in my profession.

At that time the social life was still affected by Ernest Hemingway's recent presence there. His second wife, née Pauline Pfeiffer, was still in residence that winter: she occupied their charming Spanish colonial house (which has now been converted into a museum where scandalous innuendos are whispered by the custodians about Mr. Hemingway's alleged profligate private life).

It was still a mecca for painters and writers in 1941. I met the poet Elizabeth Bishop and artist Grant Wood there that winter, and Arnold Blanch and his wife.

These things made no difference in Key West; perhaps they don't anywhere now.

There was a genteel boardinghouse called The Trade

This essay appeared in *Harper's Bazaar*, January, 1973.

Winds which had up- and downstairs verandahs encircling the house with a belvedere on the roof, and was constructed of solid mahogany. It was operated by a *grande dame* from Georgia, a lady of great kindliness, humor, and charm, the late Clara Black. She was an Episcopal minister's widow and when I told her that I was the grandson of one, she suddenly remembered that she had a little shack in back of the house which could be converted into living quarters for me. She made it very attractive and even installed a shower; the rent was seven dollars a week.

And since she suspected that I was inadequately fed, she entertained me often at dinner.

Her daughter, Marion Black Vaccaro, became a very close friend of mine. The Vaccaro family of New Orleans, into which she had married, owned the Standard Fruit Company, but the husband was such an alcoholic that in order to get him off booze they had to put him on ether. When he entered my cabin, as he often did when on ether, I would be nearly anesthetized.

Unfortunately this family has passed away now, except for a brother of Marion's, George Black, who lives in Coconut Grove and I think that he will forgive me for these irresistible reminiscences.

Regis Vaccaro had a glass eye, and one night at dinner, for no apparent reason, he snatched it out of its socket and hurled it at Mrs. Black. It landed in her soup plate. Being a true lady, she made no exhibition of dismay at this rather Bohemian gesture. She simply fished the glass eye out of her soup and gave it to Marion in a soup spoon with the casual remark, "I think that Regis lost something."

And then there was the evening when the professional gamblers of Key West, wide open as a frontier town in those days, had threatened to shoot Regis down on sight if he didn't settle some enormous debt which he couldn't settle because his family kept him on a generous but limited allowance; we had to put him on the floor of an old Ford owned by a friend of mine and drive him off the Keys at breakneck speed after dark. The radiator started to leak but this did not phase Miss Clara. She had us fill it with sea water continually till we reached the safe distance of a friend's house in Coconut Grove.

This sort of thing was not then, and would not even be now, a particularly surprising incident in the social life of Key West.

It is still a haven for those who choose to drop out of conventional society.

It is now the final retreat of "the flower children," and Monroe County, to which Key West belongs, was probably carried by Senator McGovern.

Is there a new word for "hippies"? It hardly matters if there is or not, since they appear the same, and the main street of Key West, Duval, is almost preempted by them after midnight.

Very few of them are employed; they are very thin, almost emaciated, but with the inward serenity of young Buddhists.

One night I passed a young man leaning against a wall because he was too weak to stand unsupported.

"What's the matter, son?"

"I need a place to crash. You see, I just got back from

South America where I got this amoebic dysentery thing."

"Have you been treated for it?"

"No, man, you know you can't be treated, just diagnosed if you're lucky, but with no bread, who is about to treat you?"

His large, translucent eyes, sunk in deep shadow, betrayed no disturbance over his circumstance.

Key West is like that. It always was and still is.

Sometimes I think most of the kids live on pure air, and the air is the purest I have breathed in the States.

There is still an artists' and writers' colony and there is still a great deal of indigenous, inbred eccentricity among the old "Conch" families of English origin, the first settlers.

Perhaps the preeminent writer is James Leo Herlihy, author of *Midnight Cowboy* and other distinguished novels.

There is a highly original architect, Dan Stirrup, whose style is a combination of Polynesian and contemporary. He did a kitchen for me with a stained glass window, which would have been suitable for a Catholic chapel. At first, I was distressed with a stained glass window in the kitchen, but then I found the morning light coming through it gave me an uplift for work.

There are still outstanding painters such as Edie Kidd and her late husband, Hari Kidd. I speak of him as still being here because his paintings live on in Edie's house beside the charming graveyard.

In winter, there is the explosion of the fantastic painter Henry Faulkner on the scene, never with less than a truckload of dogs and cats. He seldom passes a police car or a fire station without shouting, "Hello, girls!"—Response? Surprisingly genial.

There is a fabulously successful silkscreen factory called Key West Fabrics. It was founded by a pair of youths who had served as escorts for the late great Tallulah Bankhead. She and Miriam Hopkins, who is also the late as well as the great, were among the important visitors in time past, which has a lovely habit of remaining time present in Key West.

I have entertained the great English director Peter Hall and his dancer wife in my little Key West compound, and at this very moment, my guest house is occupied by a veteran of Vietnam, twenty-five years old, who is the most talented young writer I have met in half a lifetime.

Remember the name: Robert Carroll.

I have mentioned the indigenous eccentricities of the Conches. The town has more than its fair share of recluses. On nights of full moon, ambulance and police sirens are heard almost as continually as the baying of dogs. . . .

Now please don't hurry down here: the island has finally run out of coral-rock extensions into the sea. Almost no one plays bridge and there is almost nothing at all to do but drink or swim or—.

The Pleasures of the Table

MY FAVORITE cuisine has been Italian, not since my mother
first opened a can of Campbell's spaghetti in St. Louis fifty-
some years ago, but since I began spending so much time in
Rome in the late Forties till the early Sixties. It's more the atmosphere and the wine (Frascati produced in the Albion
Hills) of the Roman restaurants that I enjoyed, and it wasn't
the elegant ones, excellent as they were, but the little *tavernas*
that pleased me most. I remember especially a *taverna* on the
Via Margutta, close to the Spanish Steps. The Via Margutta is
full of artists, many of whom patronized this *taverna*. It had a
seductively dim atmosphere, the proprietor was cordial in a casual way, never obtrusively bustling and booming about. And
the Frascati, served in sweat-beaded carafes, offered an instant
relief from the usually blazing plaza. It was near American
Express, where I received mail, and I enjoyed a friend's letter

This appreciation was written in 1978, intended for the "Pleasures" column
of *Saturday Review*.

[165]

far more in this retreat. Often I would scribble bits of verse or dialogue on the backs of the envelopes. The food was not spectacular but good: my favorite dish was *risotto con funghi* (rice with mushrooms).

Closest to my first and most memorable apartment in Rome was a restaurant called Capriccio's, much more elegant and expensive and notable chiefly for its waiters, the most charming of whom was transferred (I refuse to say elevated) to the Savoy Grill in London.

Just off the Via Veneto was a lovely garden restaurant, Alfredo's, which had gourmet cuisine but whose special attraction (for me) was an elderly singer-guitarist with a soft, true tenor and a preference for romantic old love songs which he'd enhance with a wistful air of remembering treasures of which time had deprived him.

In Paris I liked best the little sidewalk restaurants along the (Left Bank) Boulevard Saint-Germain, through the vine-clad trellises of which you could observe the evening promenade of intriguing types bound for the Café Flore or the Deux Maggots.

In Venice I recall most fondly Harry's Bar near the Piazza San Marco and the Grand Canal restaurant of the Gritti Palace, both of which figured prominently in the later Hemingway novels.

In New York there's *Elaine's,* way up on the East Side, a celebrity hangout which is sensitively managed by its proprietress. In the difficult Sixties, Elaine would comment sympathetically on my appearance whenever I entered. If I got through the tables without collisions, she'd remark, "Well, you seem better tonight."

Perhaps the most ornate Italian restaurant in Manhattan is one to which I was recently introduced by my old friends, the sculptor Tony Smith, and his beautiful wife, the actress-singer Jane Lawrence. It's called Nanni Al Valletto, and its big menu (a copy of which I have confiscated) is adorned with a colorprint of Caravaggio's *Bacco Adolescente*.

Just opposite my hotel in Manhattan is Mario's Villa Borghese, with a particularly affable maître d' and an alcove which is ideal for professional consultation.

La Cote Basque is the only restaurant where I've truly enjoyed eating fish. And I've never encountered there the society folk that Capote attributes to it nor overheard any scandalous conversations: perhaps I have lunch too early or am too absorbed in talk at my own table.

Here in Key West, on May Day, most restaurants are closed for the hot season, and I lunch and dine in my swim trunks at my rustic patio table, totally informal with crazy conversation, no risk of being asked to autograph a catsup-stained paper napkin, and plenty of imported wines, a crate of them delivered as a parting gift by my dear friend Bob Fosse.

The Misunderstandings and Fears of an Artist's Revolt

WHY DO THEY exist, upon what plausible basis, from what do they spring?

No rational, grown-up artist deludes himself with the notion that his inherent, instinctive rejection of the ideologies of failed governments, or power-combines that mask themselves as governments, will in the least divert these monoliths from a fixed course toward the slag-heap remnants of once towering cities.

They are hell-bent upon it, and such is the force of their unconscious deathwish that if all the artists and philosophers should unite to oppose them, by this opposition they could only enact a somewhat comical demonstration, suitable for the final two minutes of a television newscast: desperate farmers driving their pigs and goats up the stately Capitol steps would be scarcely more consequential.

Written in Key West in the spring of 1978, this essay sums up Tennessee Williams's feelings about the condition of the world where we all live.

Everywhere tiny bands of terrorists Begin the beguine. In the year 2013 it has been estimated that world population will be doubled. And then?

We do not wish to destroy. We are powerless to prevent.

Young, we may shout: we receive no reply but an echo.
Old, we know, and know better. . . .
In our maturity and our age, what is there for use to do but to seek out places of quiet in which to continue our isolated cave-drawings.
Surely this is known, if anything is known by the mono-liths in their (mindless or inscrutable) ongoing.

The question becomes a useless repetition.
Why the misunderstandings and why the fears?
It seems that somehow fear can exist in a monolith with a deathwish: they may not want it spoken by those who still have tongues.
Perhaps we have mentioned some dangerous deceptions, in our time, and so are regarded as criminal offenders. . . .

What implements have we but words, images, colors, scratches upon the caves of our solitude?
In our vocations, we own no plowshares that we can beat into swords, and in our time, swords are used only for gen-tlemanly fencing in sports clubs or by actors in swashbuckling epics of the screen.

In a California interview I remember once making a statement that has, in retrospect, a somewhat pontifical ring, but the essential meaning of which I'm not inclined to retract. What I said was that civilization, at least as a long-term prospect, had ceased to exist with the first nuclear blasts at Hiroshima and Nagasaki.

I have heard it said that multitudes of "American lives" were saved by these barbaric actions.

And yet I have also heard (I believe it has been officially acknowledged) that the Japanese were attempting to negotiate an all but unconditional surrender before our military command (including the genial Mr. Truman) chose to play games with our new toy, the kind of toy that belonged in, and never should have emerged from the Devil's workshop, a toy that may eventually extinguish all intelligent life yet known to exist in the expanding (or contracting?) bubble of the cosmos.

Through my studio skylight, no sign of daybreak has appeared, but workhours have grown shorter.

With the providence of luck—redundancy deserved—I'll continue after. . . .

After?—Some hours of sleep and now again, through the skylight of my studio which, half seriously, I call "The Madhouse," another morning's ineffable beginning, pale, very pale, but apparently unclouded. Very soon, I suspect, the rising sun will reveal once again the fathomlessness of blue.

Beginning again, it is the word "Patience" that comes into my head, and what it means to artists in revolt.

By digging in and under, they may pursue their vocation of still giving you words which they hope contain truths.

Hope? I believe they still have it.

I believe they believe more hopefully than their rulers.

Especially when they are old.

They observe while they can, the confused, the fatally wrong moves of men not often evil, themselves, but forced by vested power to give support to evil.

It would seem that our childhood myths of One called God in constant combat with one called Lucifer, were an ingenuously incarnated but none the less meaningful concept of the all-pervading dilemma.

It has been said by a sophist that truth is at the bottom of a bottomless well.

Many things have been said that have the ring of a clever epigram: fashionably cynical, yet of what use?

Oh, so many, many things have been said in a tone of graceful defeat. . . . And there is no misunderstanding nor fear of that tone and those sayings.

And so I presume to insist there must be somewhere truth to be pursued each day with words that are misunderstood and feared because they are the words of an Artist, which must always remain a word most compatible with the word Revolutionary, and so be more than a word.

Therefore from youth into age I have continued and will still continue the belief and the seeking, until that time when time can no longer concern me.